ROUTLEDGE LIBRARY EDITIONS: BRITISH IN INDIA

Volume 10

GANDHI, NEHRU AND MODERN INDIA

GANDHI, NEHRU AND MODERN INDIA

ELIZABETH MAUCHLINE ROBERTS

Routledge
Taylor & Francis Group
LONDON AND NEW YORK

First published in 1974 by Methuen Educational Ltd

This edition first published in 2017
by Routledge
2 Park Square, Milton Park, Abingdon, Oxon OX14 4RN

and by Routledge
711 Third Avenue, New York, NY 10017

Routledge is an imprint of the Taylor & Francis Group, an informa business

© 1974 E. M. Roberts

All rights reserved. No part of this book may be reprinted or reproduced or utilised in any form or by any electronic, mechanical, or other means, now known or hereafter invented, including photocopying and recording, or in any information storage or retrieval system, without permission in writing from the publishers.

Trademark notice: Product or corporate names may be trademarks or registered trademarks, and are used only for identification and explanation without intent to infringe.

British Library Cataloguing in Publication Data
A catalogue record for this book is available from the British Library

ISBN: 978-1-138-22929-7 (Set)
ISBN: 978-1-315-20179-5 (Set) (ebk)
ISBN: 978-1-138-24366-8 (Volume 10) (hbk)
ISBN: 978-1-138-29061-7 (Volume 10) (pbk)

Publisher's Note
The publisher has gone to great lengths to ensure the quality of this reprint but points out that some imperfections in the original copies may be apparent.

Disclaimer
The publisher has made every effort to trace copyright holders and would welcome correspondence from those they have been unable to trace.

Gandhi, Nehru and modern India

Elizabeth Mauchline Roberts

Methuen

First published 1974
by Methuen Educational Ltd
11 New Fetter Lane, London EC4
© 1974 by E. M. Roberts

ISBN 0 423 42300 2 (Library edition)
ISBN 0 423 42390 8 (School edition)

All rights reserved.
No part of this publication may be
reproduced, stored in a retrieval system,
or transmitted in any form or by any means,
electronic, mechanical, photocopying,
recording or otherwise without the prior
permission of the publisher.

This title is available in both hardbound and
paperback editions. The paperback edition
is sold subject to the condition that it shall
not, by way of trade or otherwise, be lent,
re-sold, hired out, or otherwise circulated
without the publisher's prior consent, in any
form of binding or cover other than that in
which it is published and without a similar
condition including this condition being
imposed on the subsequent purchaser.

Contents

1 Indian background   5

2 Gandhi and the Indian nationalist movement to 1920   14

3 Jawarharlal Nehru   28

4 The struggle for independence 1920–47   32

5 Nehru's India   56

6 India and the world   83

7 Epilogue   91

    A select booklist   92

    Index   94

Acknowledgements

Permission to reproduce illustrations is gratefully acknowledged to Camera Press for numbers 1, 4, 26, 29, 34 and 36; the Radio Times Hulton Picture Library for numbers 2, 3, 5, 7, 8, 10, 12, 13, 15, 17, 18, 20, 23 and 28; the Paul Popper Photographic Agency for numbers 6, 9, 14, 16, 22, 25, 27, 30, 31, 33 and 37; the Keystone Press Agency for numbers 11, 19, 21 and 24.

1 Indian background

Introduction
This book is an account of twentieth-century India. It describes India's struggle for independence from British rule and the achievement of that independence in 1947 with the accompanying partition of India. It examines some of the political, social and economic problems facing India and the possible solutions to these problems. No book about these topics could be complete without an account of the lives and work of the two men who have done so much to fashion contemporary India: Gandhi and Nehru.

India is a land of enormous diversity and complexity. It is a very large country (the seventh largest in the world), having an area of 1 138 814 square miles (which is about twenty times the size of England and Wales). It is 2000 miles from the north to the south of India and about 1800 miles from east to west at its widest point.

The races of India
The visitor to India notices how different from each other the Indian people are. They wear a great variety of costumes. Hindu women (see page 6) wear a *sari*, Muslim women usually wear trousers and a tunic, or they might wear a *burkha* if they are in *purdah* (see page 10). This is an all-enveloping garment from head to toe with only two eye holes. Men wear tight or baggy trousers (we have taken the words *jodhpurs* and *pyjamas* from Indian words), or a kind of draped skirt of any length called a *dhoti*. With any of these they can wear a long upper garment like a night shirt, or a tight-fitting coat reaching to the knees, or just nothing at all. Many men of course wear western clothes.

There is a great variety of races in India. Many Indians especially in the northern and central areas are descended from the Aryan invaders who came to India from Asia from about 1500 BC onwards. Their descendants have paler skins than southern Indians and also tend to be taller. The Aryans conquered and drove the Dravidians, the original inhabitants of India, into the south.

In the remote areas of India there are some tribes numbering about 30 million people who live in Stone Age conditions. Some are Aborigine descendants of the first inhabitants of India. One primitive group is the Uralis of Kerala, who hunt with bows and arrows and who live in tree tops. In the north-east there are many Mongoloid people with yellow skins and slanting eyes.

Indians are even less united linguistically than they are racially. There are fifteen main languages and at least 850 different dialects and subsidiary languages of which 225 are distinct languages. All these different languages belong to four distinct groups. The northern languages are derived from the ancient language Sanskrit. In this group the most important is Hindi, India's official language and spoken by nearly 50 per cent of the population. Then there are

1 This village schoolmaster is wearing a *dhoti* and his wife is wearing a *sari*

the southern languages, the languages of the north-east, and a small group of Aborigine languages.

If four Indians speaking a language from each of these four groups met together and each spoke only his own language, they would be as mutually incomprehensible as a Japanese, a Russian, an Arab and an Englishman speaking together.

The religions of India
The religion of the great majority of Indians is Hinduism. It developed in a long period from about 1500 BC to 500 BC. It did not develop from the teachings of one prophet but gradually evolved out of Indian life.

Hinduism is a very flexible religion and does not have the rigid beliefs of, for example, Christianity. The basic belief of Hindus is the oneness of creation. God is everywhere, in everything and in everyone. The devout Hindu's aim is to achieve mystical union with God. But the Hindu also believes that there are many ways of achieving union with God and therefore different religions are but different ways of reaching the same destination. This belief makes Hindus tolerant both of other religions and of the greatest diversity of belief in Hinduism itself. Some Hindus worship one God, others believe that there is one God but that he has many forms and that each has a separate name and identity.

Hindus believe in the transmigration of souls. That is, a person's soul survives the death of his body and is reborn into another body. If a man or a woman has lived virtuously, he or she will be born again into a better life. If he has led a bad life he will be reborn into a lower caste. Those who continue to be reborn into higher and higher castes will eventually achieve union with God and then cease to be reborn.

This belief has resulted in two very important basic elements in Hindu society. Firstly, Hindus have concentrated on preparing themselves for the next world. They carry out endless religious rituals, spending time in prayer and contemplation and giving alms to the poor in preference to attempting to alter the material conditions of this world. This is one of the primary reasons for India's historical and present poverty.

Secondly, this belief has cemented the caste system into Hinduism. The caste into which one is born is regarded as either a reward or a punishment for one's actions in a previous life. A caste is a group of families who can intermarry and eat together without being polluted. Members of a caste are allowed to follow only a certain number of occupations, and in some sub-castes members follow only one occupation.

Originally there were four castes. At the top were the Brahmins or priests, who studied and knew the rightful path in life. Secondly there were the Ksatriyas or warriors, whose duty was to fight and rule.

2 Delhi, 1946: an Untouchable woman washes her feet in a filthy gutter

Thirdly there were the Vaisyas, merchants and craftsmen. Fourthly there were the Sudras or peasants. Gradually these castes were divided and subdivided. In some cases the sub-castes have become ridiculous: there is a caste for the potters who use a big wheel and one for those using a small wheel, with total segregation between the two castes.

At the bottom of the caste system are the 50 million Untouchables. Over the centuries they have been expected to do all the menial 'unclean' tasks such as cleaning the streets, handling dead animals, sewage disposal and laundry work. Untouchables have had to live apart from other people as their touch and even their shadow were thought to pollute Hindus of other castes. They were forbidden to enter Hindu temples, draw water from wells or even walk on the roads. (Their position has been altered in recent years: see pages 61 and 80.

The ritual rules of Hinduism in general and of each caste in particular affect every aspect of a man's life: what work he does, whom he marries, what he eats and what he eats off, when he washes and how he washes, when and how his hair is cut and where he will travel. The number of choices open to a Hindu are infinitely fewer than those a western European can make.

A westerner may well wonder why so many Indians have accepted the caste system. Each caste has or had a Panchayat or court to punish caste members who break the caste rules. An offender might be sentenced to a fine or a ritual bath to cleanse him from his pollution. But in serious cases a man and his family could be sentenced to expulsion from the caste. This was a terrible punishment. Gandhi's niece never forgave him for crossing the seas, a 'crime' for which the whole family was expelled from the caste. Thus the niece could not marry anyone in the caste or visit her friends' houses or eat with them. She died in bitter, lonely isolation.

There have been various attempts to reform and reinterpret Hinduism when it has become unintelligible to ordinary people. Two men in particular attempted to reform Hinduism and instead founded two new religions. Mahavira (540–467 BC) founded Jainism. There are about 2 million Jains in India now. Buddha (567–487 BC) founded Buddhism. There are about 4 million Buddhists practising today.

Islam
The Muslim invaders who first started arriving in the eighth century and who established the first Muslim Empire in the twelfth century introduced their religion into India. There are now very large numbers of Muslims in western and northern India (an estimated 50 million in 1964) and in Pakistan. There are also millions in Bangladesh. These are mostly the decendants of Indian Hindus who were converted by force to Islam. Muslim beliefs are very different from those of Hindus. They believe in one God, Allah, and despise all idols and idol worship (which they believe Hindus practise). They are fierce about their religion and believe in converting others to their faith. They believe in the equality of all men (but *not* women!) and therefore fiercely denounce the caste system. They are meat eaters while the majority of Hindus are vegetarians, and certainly those who do eat meat would never eat the flesh of their sacred cows.

One of the great differences in social attitudes between Muslims and Hindus is their attitude to women. Hindus have always greatly respected women; unfortunately through the centuries this respect tended to develop into masculine over-protectiveness and Hindu women found little scope for their energies outside the home. But within the home they usually ruled supreme, running the lives of male and female members alike. In Muslim households women play a secondary role to men. Until recently they were not allowed to leave their homes either unveiled or unaccompanied. This strict seclusion is called *purdah*.

Christians
The Christians are descended from converts made at various times during the last 2000 years. The Church is South India was founded by St Thomas.

In the last 400 years other Christian missionaries have come to India from Portugal, France and Great Britain. In 1965 there were 11 million Christians in India.

Sikhs
The Sikh religion was founded by a Hindu called Guru (Great Teacher) Nanak (1469–1538) who drew his ideas from both Muslims and Hindus. He preached the equality of all men and women. He believed that there is only one God, who is worshipped by all men in all religions. Nanak opposed the caste system and all idolatry. He formed his followers into a tightly knit military brotherhood, pledged to resist the Muslim conquerors. The Sikhs became the

3 Muslim women wearing the *burkha*

rulers of an area of north-west India, the Punjab. This was conquered by the British in the nineteenth century. The Sikhs have retained their military prowess and have served with great distinction in both the British and the Indian armies. They are also skilful farmers and engineers and traders. Male Sikhs do not cut their hair, which is covered by a turban. There are 10 million Sikhs in India today.

The Parsees
The Parsees are few in number but influential. They are descendants of eighth-century refugees from Persia. Their religion includes the worship of fire.

They have made great contributions to industry, education, science and politics. The great Tata Iron and Steel Company at Jamshedpur was founded by a Parsee, J. N. Tata. The Prime Minister of India, Mrs Indira Ghandi, married a Parsee, Feroze, who died in 1961. (He was not related to Mahatma Gandhi.) In 1965 there were 100 000 Parsees in India.

The political situation in India in 1900
From the sixteenth century onwards western European powers showed interest in India, then ruled by the Muslim Mogul Emperor. India was the source of spices, valuable jewels, precious metals and works of art.

Gradually these traders and their governments became more and more involved in Indian political affairs, as local rulers either quarrelled amongst themselves or with the Mogul Emperor. The English defeated their main rivals in India, the French, in the middle of the eighteenth century and gradually, with the collapse of the Mogul Empire, came to rule more and more of India.

By 1900 the political situation in India was as follows. Firstly there were the 562 princely states (see Map A). They acknowledged the suzerainty (overlordship)

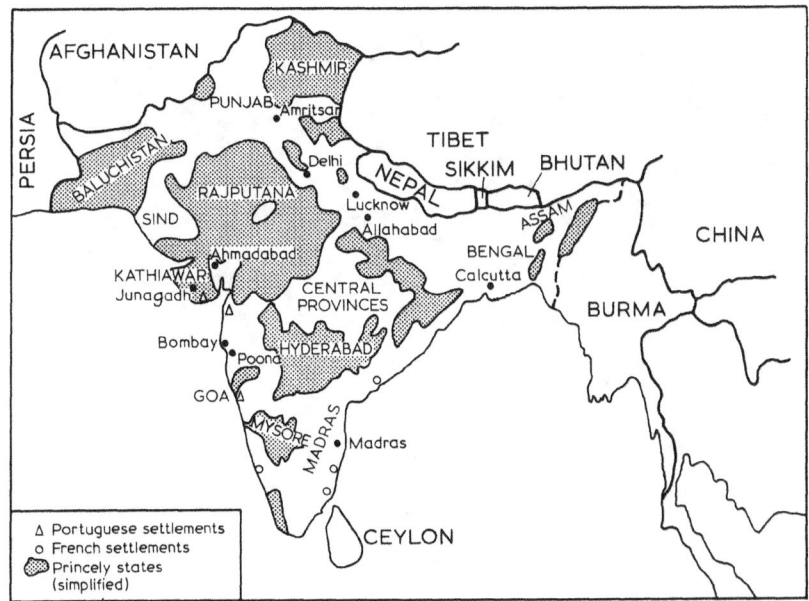

Map A The Indian empire before 1947

of the British, who managed their foreign affairs and their relations with other Indian states. Each prince had a British adviser, whose power depended both on his own and the prince's personalities. On the whole the princes were dealt with very gently by the British, who remembered the part some Indians had played in the great Indian Mutiny in 1857 and therefore feared another princely rebellion. Most of them enjoyed British support. They feared and opposed the end of British rule and curried favour with the British by putting down any unrest in their states. The 562 princely states covered about one-third of India and contained one-quarter of the population. They varied enormously in size. Hyderabad was bigger than England and Wales put together (it covered 32 000 square miles). In Kathiawar (Gandhi's home area) there were over 200 tiny states. One had only 900 people and an area of less than ten square miles. On the whole the princes ruled their subjects harshly.

The rest of India was ruled directly by the British. It was divided into provinces, each with an English Governor. In 1861 Legislative Councils (law-making bodies) were created both for the central government and for each province. Some Indians were chosen by the British to sit on these councils.

The laws made by the provincial councils had to be approved by the Viceroy, the Queen's representative in India. The final word on Indian affairs rested with the Secretary of State in London, who was responsible to the British Cabinet and Parliament. In 1876 Queen Victoria became Empress of India and from that date until

4 An Indian prince rides to his wedding. This photograph was taken in 1970

1947, when the British King stopped being Emperor, you can see on British coins the words 'Ind. Imp.' – *Indiae Imperator*.

An English Prime Minister in the nineteenth century, Disraeli, once called the Indian Empire 'the brightest jewel of the British Crown'. Very few Englishmen in 1900 would have disagreed with him. The English had a glamorous but vague picture of India, with jungles and tiger hunts, huge tea plantations, princes decked with jewels riding on elaborately decorated elephants, beautiful graceful women wearing vivid *saris*, the Taj Mahal by moonlight, and pilgrims washing themselves in the sacred Ganges.

The British took great pride in the benefits brought by their rule to India. There was less violence than before. The country had been rid of the blood-thirsty *thuggee*, who roamed around in bands ritually strangling travellers as part of their perverted religion. The Indian Civil Service, which attracted some of the best of British brains, acted with great integrity bringing justice to all. By 1900 the British had built 25 000 miles of railways and 70 000 miles of canals. Fourteen million acres of land were irrigated and most of the all too frequent outbreaks of typhoid, cholera, plague and famine were quickly brought under control by the British. The British also brought education and, by 1900, 23 000 Indians were in Indian universities and many more were in hundreds of schools.

There were, however, many bad things about British rule in India. Far too many Britons in India antagonised the native population by treating them as inferiors whatever their education, career or social status. Often they were denied entry to British homes and clubs.

Economically India suffered from British rule. Many farmers were encouraged to grow raw materials for the British which were used in British industries and the profits were sent to Great Britain. Usually, however, the raw materials were exported to Britain, which meant that fewer farmers grew food and therefore there was less for the population to eat. The British expected India to buy British manufactured goods. The importing of British cotton cloth ruined the Indian village textile workers. Other imports prevented the growth of other Indian manufacturing industries, for example, the metal work and shipbuilding industries. All the industrial products needed for building the railways were imported from Britain, so there was no possibility of developing Indian iron, steel, coal and engineering industries. In fact, in the years before 1900 there was an actual decline in the number of Indian industrial workers.

By 1900 there was amongst both intellectuals and ordinary people much disillusionment with British rule. This disillusionment was to grow into demands for an end to British rule and the establishment of Indian independence.

2 Gandhi and the Indian nationalist movement to 1920

Gandhi's early life and education
Mohandas Karamchand Gandhi was born on 2nd October 1869 into a Hindu family of the Vaisya caste (see page 8). His father and grandfather had been Prime Ministers in various tiny states of the Kathiawar peninsula on the shores of the Arabian Sea. The family was far from wealthy, but the children never knew the dreadful poverty of the great mass of their fellow countrymen. There were four Gandhi children, three boys and a girl, and Mohan, being the youngest, tended to be spoiled.

The children respected their father but adored their mother, Putlibai, and from her Mohan learned much of his religion. She was a devout Hindu and as part of her religion fasted regularly. One of Mohan's earliest memories of his mother was of her fasting during the rainy season and vowing not to eat until she had seen the sun. The anxious children continually scanned the sky: 'Mother,' they called, 'come quickly and look, the sun is shining, now you can eat.' Putlibai came out, but the sun had gone behind a cloud, so she shook her head and said cheerfully, 'God did not want me to eat today.' Mohan learned that religion was not a mournful thing because Putlibai was always so cheerful, especially when fasting.

Mohan went to school when he was five, a shy little boy whose ears stuck out. He did not enjoy school, finding difficulty with things like multiplication tables, and he lived in permanent fear of his classmates' teasing.

Gandhi's teenage life was rather different from that of a teenager in western Europe. He was married at the age of thirteen, but he continued to be very much under his parents' domination. His bride, Kasturbai, was chosen by his parents.

Marriage was not quite what Mohan expected; and in his later life he campaigned against the custom of child marriage. In his innocence, Mohan had thought it would be nice to have a girl to play with, but once he was married he fell passionately in love with Kasturbai. Unhappily he was not mature enough to cope with his emotions. He became insanely jealous if Kasturbai went out by herself, but Kasturbai, alternately smiling or weeping, did exactly as she liked; she infuriated Mohan but unintentionally gave him his first lessons in the effectiveness of passive resistance. His passion for Kasturbai was so obsessional that he was unable to concentrate on his studies; as he was a far from brilliant student this was serious.

Like many Hindu families the Gandhis were vegetarians, but Mohan learned a rhyme at school:

> Behold the mighty Englishman,
> He rules the Indian small,
> Because being a meat eater,
> He is five cubits tall.

Urged on by a friend Mohan started to eat

meat. He went to restaurants and had meat meals and then had to invent elaborate reasons why he could not eat his meals at home. Eventually he abandoned meat eating because it resulted in continual lying; already the habit of telling the truth was so ingrained that lying was a mental agony to him. He also experimented with smoking, stealing money from the servants to buy cigarettes. Eventually he and his friend, tired of the necessity of seeking parental approval for any activity in which they wanted to take part, decided on suicide. They collected some poisonous berries, but who would eat them first? Would the agony be terrible? Eventually to prove their courage they ate two berries and to their enormous relief nothing happened.

When Gandhi was sixteen his father died and Kasturbai had their first child, who also died. These two blows almost broke Mohan's heart, but he matured rapidly and could no longer be called a child. In his grief he began his lifelong search for spiritual and religious truth.

Gandhi matriculated from school, with rather poor marks, when he was eighteen. The family discussed at length what was best for him to do. The men of the family decided that he should become a lawyer, but to do so he would have to go to England. Gandhi accepted this decision, but it was not easy; it meant that the family became outcasts from their caste.

5 Gandhi as a law student in England, about 1887

Mohan vowed to keep his religion and stay faithful to Kasturbai. He found this vow gave him the moral strength to resist the many temptations he encountered. He continued throughout his life to believe that sacred vows gave a person the moral strength to do what was right. During his stay in London and through his legal studies, Gandhi developed an admiration for British justice and British laws that was to remain with him for a very long time. But his stay in London did not make him a brown-skinned Englishman. At first he tried various western ways, dressing in a 'frock' coat with a top hat, and taking lessons in the violin, elocution, dancing and French. Gradually he gave up trying to become an English gentleman and developed patterns of thought and behaviour which remained with him all his life.

Under the influence of vegetarians and books about vegetarianism, he came to believe that rearing animals for their flesh is cruel, unnecessary and degrading. Man is more like the fruit-eating ape than a carnivore and is therefore likelier to be healthy if he does not eat meat. He became more and more interested in the 'simple life' and managed to live very frugally on the equivalent of 6p per day.

Gandhi looked again at his faith and for the first time read the *Gita* (the Hindu holy book). He was impressed with its emphasis on the need for the continual search for truth. He also read the New Testament and found the phrase 'Resist not evil' meaningful.

After three years in London, Gandhi qualified as a barrister and returned home; but he was not happy. Putlibai, his beloved mother, had died in his absence; there was still tension between him and Kasturbai; and worst of all he could not find work. Despite his experiences of living abroad and meeting many people, he was too nervous to speak in court. Fewer and fewer people asked him to take on their cases and in his despair he again thought about suicide. Then, through family connections, he was asked to go to South Africa for a year to act in a lawsuit involving a firm of wealthy Indian merchants.

Gandhi felt he must go, if he was ever to make a living to support his family (he now had a second son). This decision altered his whole life.

Gandhi's years in South Africa
South Africa was an unhappy country, its people divided into mutually suspicious and hostile groups: there were the Boers, the English, the Africans, who were in the vast majority, the coloured people of mixed racial origin, and the Indians. The majority of Indians were indentured labourers, who had been persuaded to go to South Africa to improve their standard of living. They had to serve their master for five years and then they were 'freed'. Often they found themselves in a state near to slavery, underfed, uneducated and very poor.

Gandhi realised that there was one burden shared by all non-white South Africans, and that was colour prejudice. Three days after his arrival he was ejected from court where he was acting as a barrister because he refused to remove his turban. A little later he had to make a journey to Pretoria in the Transvaal. Although he had bought a first-class railway ticket, a white passenger insisted that he was removed to the luggage van. When Gandhi protested the guard unceremoniously deposited him on the next railway station and threw his luggage after him. The nightmare journey was continued by stage coach, where he was beaten up by one passenger for refusing

6 Gandhi as the prosperous lawyer in South Africa

to crouch on a pile of filthy sacks at the driver's feet (despite having paid for an inside seat); five hotels in Johannesburg refused him a room because he was an Indian; and by the time he reached Pretoria, Gandhi had decided that he would fight racial prejudice wherever he found it. Gandhi, the nervous, stammering little lawyer, was now transformed into a courageous fighter and leader. There was plenty for him to fight.

In 1885 the government of the Transvaal had declared that Indians could not vote in elections or acquire citizenship; the other states had similar repressive legislation. The Transvaal even forbade non-whites to walk on the pavement, and Gandhi himself, ignoring this law, was once kicked into the gutter.

Although his court case was finished in a year Gandhi stayed in South Africa until 1915, paying only short visits to India, the first of which (in 1896) was to bring Kasturbai and his two little boys to South Africa. He worked as a lawyer and built up very successful legal practices, but almost all his earnings went to his good causes, as he continued to pursue his simple life.

Gandhi knew that if the Indians were ever to make their voices heard by the government in South Africa, they must have self-respect. If they wanted equality, they had to demonstrate that they were equal to white people. So Gandhi insisted, as he was to do all his life, on the utmost cleanliness in Indian homes, personally inspecting them on many occasions. Secondly he believed that to be effective, the Indians had to be united. He had a wonderful, almost magical, ability to unite people whatever their background, helping them to forget their differences of religion, caste, colour or wealth. Slowly but surely he built up his Natal Indian Congress.

Whenever he could, Gandhi fought racial prejudice through the courts, almost always winning his cases. But gradually he realised that despite his respect for the law and the legal processes of the courts, there were times when it was right to break the law. Gradually he developed his philosophy of *satyagraha*: this has often been inaccurately translated as 'passive resistance', 'civil disobedience' or 'non-violent non-cooperation'. Perhaps the best translation is 'firmness in truth' or truth force.

The people who practised *satyagraha* were called *satyagrahis*. Before they could act correctly in any situation, they had to see the truth of that situation and recognise clearly the evil in it. Truth could only be perceived if the mind was loving and free from all hatred and prejudice. Once truth was discovered, the *satyagrahi* must act.

Gandhi was always as concerned with the *means* of combating evil as with the *end* of overcoming it. The end never justified the means for Gandhi, therefore the *satyagrahi* must always be non-violent.

Satyagrahis could use boycotts and strikes, but when authority moved against them they had to submit to blows without retaliating, and go to prison or even death without rancour. Ultimately the opposition would be impressed by the *satyagrahis'* courage and willingness to suffer for their cause and would then see that justice was done. It has always been argued that Gandhi's *satyagraha* could only succeed if his opponents had moral scruples and a conscience. It certainly was successful in both South Africa and India, and Gandhi used it as a political weapon several times.

In 1913 the South African* Supreme Court declared that all Hindu, Muslim and Parsee marriages were invalid. Thus at one stroke Indians' wives were declared concubines and their children bastards.

The Indians were incensed and Gandhi found a new and powerful weapon in his hands: the determination of Indian women to see justice done. Henceforward they played a major part in all Gandhi's campaigns. The Congress Movement was so strengthened that Gandhi felt able to threaten the South African Prime Minister, General Smuts, with two new weapons. If nothing was done about Indian grievances, there would be a mass refusal to pay the Indian tax and Indian indentured labourers would be called out on strike.

The government refused to act, and a group of women went into the Natal coalfield to persuade the miners to come out on strike. The women were arrested, but this so enraged the men that they struck in force. Gandhi organised a mass march and the government reacted with predictable violence. The prisons overflowed, Indian women were sentenced to hard labour and some died. Gandhi and other leaders were imprisoned. The police and army tried to force back the striking miners with whips and guns, but all failed.

The English government made strong representations to the South Africans. The

* In 1910 the Union of South Africa had been created, uniting the Transvaal, Natal, Cape Colony and the Orange Free State.

government collapsed; Gandhi's truth force had won. An Act of Parliament ended the special tax on Indians; their marriages were recognised as legal; Indian immigration was made easier; and the ending of the indentured labour scheme was begun.

In 1915 Gandhi left South Africa for good. Sadly, in the years after his departure the legal position of Indians steadily worsened, as indeed it did for all coloured people. Gandhi always had to face the difficult moral problem of how much suffering it was right for his followers to endure in trying to achieve what *he* wanted. At home there was a similar problem. Was it right to bring suffering to his family because of what he believed? Usually Gandhi was so sure he had recognised the truth that all he could do was to try to convice his family that he was right.

For much of the time in South Africa he and his family (there were four sons, Devadas, Harilal, Manilal and Ramdas) lived on first the Phoenix and second the Tolstoy communal farms. Gandhi continued with his experiments in diet, rejecting more and more food as being injurious to health; he finally settled on a diet entirely composed of fruit and nuts.

Gandhi's ideas (or fads as some called them) upset Kasturbai. She had been brought up to believe that an Indian home was a place of peace and privacy; now she found herself sharing it with a mass of strangers. She dearly loved traditional Indian food and resented Gandhi's ban on all spices; frequently she rose from the table famished, unable to share her husband's enthusiasm for a diet of fruit and nuts. She resented Gandhi's growing tendency to reject all material possessions. She had to take down all the curtains; worst of all, she had to return various gifts of jewellery, given by Gandhi's admirers, which she had hoped to save for her future daughters-in-law. Her husband once ordered her to empty an Untouchable's chamber-pot. She forced herself, weeping, to carry it downstairs and then suddenly shouted at Gandhi, 'Keep your house and let me go.' Forgetful of non-violence, Gandhi dragged her to the gate where she shouted at him to stop making a fool of himself in public, and he let her go. Oddly enough life became more peaceful when Gandhi took a vow of celibacy in 1906, believing that by renouncing sex he could concentrate wholly on his work. Gradually Kasturbai began to understand what Gandhi was trying to do and he was delighted when she took an active part in the *satyagraha* movement after the South African courts' decision on Indian marriages.

The founding of the Indian National Congress, and a brief outline of its activities to 1917
One of the results of the British Raj in India was the training of several thousand Indians as lawyers, doctors, journalists and teachers. Gradually groups of these middle-class

7 Gandhi and his wife Kasturbai. This photograph was taken after Gandhi and his family returned to India. It shows the simplicity of Gandhi's clothes after he adopted the 'simple life'

intellectuals saw more and more clearly the need for various reforms in India. However, the group that was to play the crucial role in the future fight for Indian independence was the Indian National Congress, established in 1885. It certainly did not begin as a political movement; it was started by Alan Octavian Hume (1829–1912), an Englishman recently retired from the Indian Civil Service.

The first Congress met in Bombay in 1885 with representatives from all parts of British India. Nearly all were either lawyers or journalists. The movement grew quickly and by 1887 there were 600 delegates, including 83 Muslims, at the annual meeting.

The members were almost embarrassingly eager to emphasise their loyalty to the British Raj. Over and over again protestations of such loyalty were made, together with grateful comments about the benefits of British rule. Three of the early Congress Presidents were Englishmen and debates were always conducted in English.

In no sense whatever could the Congress be called a revolutionary political movement in the first twenty years of its existence. Then in 1905 Congress became suddenly much more revolutionary and politically minded. The cause was the partition of Bengal. Lord Curzon, the Viceroy, believed that the province of Bengal, with a population of 78 million, was too large to administer effectively as one unit. The Bengalis, some of the most politically conscious of all Indians, believed that Curzon was trying to weaken them by a policy of 'divide and rule'. Monster protest meetings were held and a boycott of foreign goods (notably Lancashire cotton) was organised. Soon support for the Bengalis' stand came from all over India: for the very first time a crisis affecting one area of India became a matter of concern for the whole country. Indian nationalism came of age, and in 1906, Congress, as the representative of this movement, demanded for the first time Home Rule for India, or *swaraj* as they called it.

There was an election in England in 1906 and a reforming Liberal government was returned to power. The Secretary of State for India was John Morley who, together with the new Viceroy of India, Lord Minto, began to introduce reforms into India which could ultimately lead to *swaraj*. The most famous of these reforms (sometimes called the Morley-Minto reforms) was the Indian Councils Act of 1909. For the first time Indians could be elected to the provincial and local Legislative Councils in appreciable numbers. The electorate was very small, but nevertheless the principle had been established that Indians could elect other Indians to make the laws which governed them. Another important step was the ending of the partition of Bengal in 1911.

The excellent relations existing between Congress and the mass of Indian people on one side and the British on the other were further strengthened by the outbreak of the First World War in 1914. There was great loyalist feeling towards Great Britain and many Indians volunteered to fight. By 1916 a million Indian troops were fighting on the Western Front.

In 1917 the new Secretary of State for India, Sir Edwin Montague, told the British House of Commons that the British government's policy was one of increasing the part played by Indians in every branch of Indian government and of giving India more and more self-government. Eventually India would have her own government but remain part of the British Empire. Congress leaders were more than satisfied by the Montague declaration: it seemed that their policy of moderation and cooperation had succeeded and that Home Rule was very near.

Gandhi and the transformation of India and Congress 1917–20
When Gandhi returned to India in 1915, he was still a great admirer of the British. He helped the war cause by carrying out recruiting campaigns for the British army (although he did not feel able to fight himself).

At this time he had no intention of becoming involved in Indian politics although he did attend Congress and sometimes addressed public meetings. He vowed that never again would he be a lawyer. His chief concern was in founding a community where people who shared his views could also share a communal life. He called his settlement *the Satyagraha Ashram* and established it in his old home area of Gujerat near Ahmadabad. This *ashram* was to be the birthplace of modern India. Gandhi hoped to train people to go out and try to solve some of India's terrible social problems. He knew that nothing could be done unless his workers were thoroughly prepared, mentally and spiritually. All who lived on the *ashram* took many vows, which included pledges of poverty, chastity, service, truth, fearlessness, manual labour, non-violence and the rejection of Untouchability.

Gandhi was initially concerned with revitalising the Indian villages. He felt they had been ruined by western capitalism. For instance, the ancient crafts of spinning and weaving were almost entirely forgotten because generations of villagers had been encouraged to buy cheap Lancashire cotton. So Gandhi in his usual practical way insisted that all those in the *ashram* become proficient in spinning and weaving so that these crafts could be reintroduced into the villages. With this one reform Gandhi hoped to achieve much. He hoped firstly that it would stop the outflow of Indian money to Lancashire; secondly that it would provide the villages with an extra source of income and employment, for surplus cloth could be sold in the cities; thirdly that it would be a simple and easily

8 Gandhi demonstrating hand-spinning in Calcutta

understood symbol of Gandhi's belief that manual work was as important as brainwork and worthy of equal respect (he believed that too many educated Indians scorned manual work and were thus unable to help their country in the ways most needed); and fourthly that the revival of these traditional crafts would help solve the problem of India's hundreds of thousands of beggars. Beggars must be given work, not charity, for the former gave a man dignity and self-respect, the latter made him little short of an animal.

Gandhi's second self-appointed task seemed almost insuperable: it was to end Untouchability (see page 8). He called the Untouchables *'Harijans'* or 'Children of God'. First of all he had to get his own friends to accept Untouchables as equals. They still found it difficult to accept an Untouchable family into the *ashram*, even though the father had managed to acquire an education and was a teacher. The man who owned the nearby well complained that it would be polluted if the Untouchables used the water bucket. Worst of all the wealthy merchants who financed the *ashram* immediately withdrew their support. It soon seemed as if it would have to close down. When things were desperate, a miracle happened. A large black car drew up outside the *ashram* and from it stepped a stranger who handed Gandhi enough money to keep the settlement going for another year. The Untouchable family stayed and were fully accepted.

Many people meeting Gandhi for the first time were astonished, for he hardly looked like a great man. He cut his own hair (as part of the simple life) and until he became bald his bolder friends would tease him with remarks like, 'Hello, the rats been at your hair again?' As the years passed he became progressively more toothless, refusing to be fitted with false ones as they were a luxury the great majority of Indians could not afford. His face was a bright copper colour, his ears stuck out, his nose was pendulous and his chin strong and granite-like. He was most at ease in the dress he wore constantly as he grew older, a loin-cloth or *dhoti*, with a blanket as a cloak for extra warmth. This costume identified him even more closely with India's poor and again it symbolised his simple life.

As had already been seen, the year 1917 marked the high point in the relationship between Congress and the British government. India confidently expected Home Rule very soon. But the same year Gandhi became disillusioned with British rule. One day a ragged peasant arrived at the house where Gandhi was staying in Calcutta and asked him to visit the distant district of Champaran at the foot of the Himalayas, to see for himself the misery of the people there. Almost all of them worked in a state of semi-slavery for English landlords. They earned about 1p a day and each peasant had to plant three-twentieths of his land with indigo, from which purple dye was made.

There was always more than anyone wanted to buy, so the price for it was very low. When Gandhi tried to enter Champaran, to find out for himself what was wrong, the local police refused him permission. Gandhi calmly disobeyed the order, was arrested and was put on trial. He stated his case quietly and the magistrate dismissed it. As a result of the mass of evidence which Gandhi collected from thousands of peasants, the provincial government ended the obligation to plant a fixed amount of indigo and ordered the planters to return a proportion of the money extracted illegally from the peasants.

His experiences in Champaran convinced Gandhi for the first time that sooner or later the British must leave India. He himself said later, 'In Champaran I declared that the British could not order me about in my own country.' No other Indian had made such a declaration before. He had in fact conducted an individual *satyagraha* campaign.

Disillusionment with the British came to be shared by many other Indians in the years 1918–20. In 1918 a 'flu epidemic swept across India, killing at least 13 million people and leaving millions more weak and dispirited. Then the war ended in November 1918 and almost immediately the wartime prosperity of Indian industry disappeared. The army had no further need for supplies of iron, steel, coal, munitions or cloth. Production fell and unemployment rose.

Many Indians were deeply resentful. They knew that during the war Great Britain had needed Indian men and supplies. What was to be India's reward? Was it simply to be unemployment and economic recession? Should it not be an immediate granting of *swaraj*?

Then the British government passed the Government of India Act in 1919. It laid down the way India was to be governed until 1935. The most important powers still rested in British hands, but there were changes. In local affairs and in the Legislative Assembly and the Civil Service, Indian representation was increased. The franchise was enlarged, but still only 2·8 per cent of the population could vote.

Throughout the war there had been terrorist outbreaks in the Punjab because of grievances about the methods of raising men and money for the war. In 1918 the British government feared that this terrorism might spread and so appointed a committee of inquiry under the chairmanship of an English judge, Sir Sidney Rowlatt. The Rowlatt Commission recommended that judges could try political prisoners without a jury and that provincial Governors could imprison suspects without a trial. The Viceroy, despite the protests of the Indian members of the Legislative Council, converted these recommendations into the so-called Rowlatt Acts in February 1919. These Acts were in fact never used, but they created a great wave of anger throughout India.

In 1918, Tilak, the Congress leader, went to London to plead for complete provincial self-government. He was away when the Rowlatt Acts were passed, and in his absence Gandhi came to the fore in Congress. He launched a protest movement. Mass meetings were held and a national *hartal** was called when all business and work should stop. Those supporting the *hartal* were to spend the day in prayer. Many Indians as a gesture of protest returned medals and honours to the British

* A *hartal* was a strike by workers and businessmen.

9 Unemployed workers and their families in Calcutta after the First World War

government. Individual *satyagrahis* sold forbidden political pamphlets in the streets.

Gandhi, as always, intended his movement to be non-violent, but in the Punjab, with its long history of violence, a mob got out of control and murdered four Europeans in Amritsar. Gandhi, deeply grieved at what had happened, tried to enter the Punjab to restore peace. The Governor refused him permission. Gandhi then began a fast to punish himself for this violence. Meanwhile the new military commander of the Punjab, General Dyer, issued an order forbidding all further public meetings, but the order was in English and he did not trouble to see how far it was understood. On 13th April a large crowd of about 10 000 men, women and children met in an enclosed space called Jallianwallah Bagh. The General decided that the Indians must be taught a lesson. Once the square was full and the few exits blocked, without ordering the crowd to disperse, he gave his men the order to fire; the firing continued for ten minutes and only stopped when the 1650 rounds of ammunition ran out. Eventually the hysterical crowd was cleared, leaving behind on the flagstones 379 dead and 1200 wounded. One of General Dyer's subalterns spoke with relish of 'the seething mass of sweating niggers being mown down'. Nor was this the end of the horror of Amritsar: 500 students and teachers were arrested; men were publicly flogged and women tortured; in the market place a cage was built to hold the arrested people; peasants were shot; hostages were taken, their frantic relatives knew not where; water and electricity were cut off from Indian homes; and all those passing the place where an Englishwoman had been attacked had to do so on all fours like animals. All this went on for eight weeks, with the aim of crushing a revolutionary plot which had never existed.

Perhaps to Indian sensibilities the most wounding aspect of the Amritsar affair was the way in which it was treated in England. On his return to England General Dyer was presented with a jewelled sword engraved with 'Saviour of the Punjab'. English public opinion was largely behind Dyer, but in fact all he had done was to unite Indians as never before against the British. He had succeeded far better than any Indian politician had ever been able to do both in uniting the people and in popularising the cause of *swaraj*. Indians previously loyal to the Raj lost all faith in British justice and fair play.

Amritsar had one more vitally important consequence. Tilak was still away and Gandhi became the unquestioned leader of Congress. Thus began the Gandhian reign of twenty-eight years when Gandhi, overshadowing everyone else, led his country to independence from British rule.

3 Jawarharlal Nehru

Family background
The Nehrus are Brahmins – Kashmiri Brahmins. They are thus at the very top of the Hindu caste system, India's aristocrats. It is a Kashmir custom to call every male Brahmin 'Pundit', hence Nehru is sometimes called 'Pundit Nehru'. Despite being high-caste Hindus, the Nehru family were not very orthodox. Jawarharlal's father, Motilal Nehru, cared little for religion, nor did his son. It was left to the women of the family to preserve something of the Hindu religion.
Motilal was greatly influenced by the English people he knew. He was a barrister and very wealthy. He therefore was able to live the life of a wealthy English gentleman. In 1900 he bought a luxurious house, *Anand Bhawan* ('Abode of Happiness'), with two swimming pools (one indoor and one outdoor). He had a motor car, the first one to be imported into India, and entertained lavishly. He kept three separate kitchens for his Muslim, Hindu and English visitors, all of whom his son met.

Jawarharlal ('Red Jewel') was born in Allahabad on 14th November in 1889. Motilal was determined to bring up his son like an English gentleman, so until the age of fifteen, Jawarharlal had a series of tutors who were usually English and who taught him in English. English really was his 'natural' language (all his books were written in English and his fellow prisoners later in life said he spoke English in his sleep). He was given lessons in Urdu, Hindi and Sanskrit, but he had to have further lessons in adult life because he was so 'rusty' in Indian languages.

Nehru's mother was Swarup Rani. She had been married at thirteen and her only interests were her home and her children. She was tiny, fragile and adored her son.

Jawarharlal was an only child until he was eleven, when his sister Nan (Vijayalakshmi) was born, in 1900; another sister Betti (Krishna) was born in 1909.

The dominating force in Jawarharlal's life was his father. Jawarharlal inherited from his father an admiration for English things and people, common sense, tolerance and admiration of Muslims, and doubts about much of the Hindu religion. However, Motilal also had some bad influences on his son. He dominated him too much and left Jawarharlal often unable to make decisions without consulting his father. His lack of decisiveness continued as he grew older.

All Nehru's hobbies were those of an upper-class English boy of a similar age. He rode very often, went swimming and played cricket and tennis. He loved reading, especially the books of Lewis Carroll, Kipling, Mark Twain, Arthur Conan Doyle, Dickens, Scott and Thackeray.

Nehru in England
When Jawarharlal was fifteen Motilal decided it was time for his son to attend school. Not unexpectedly he wanted him to have the best of British education. So Jawarharlal was sent to Harrow.

10 Nehru at Harrow in 1907

Then he went to Cambridge to spend three peaceful and blissfully happy years, studying natural sciences: chemistry, geology and botany. He had many other interests. He watched what was happening in British politics, was fascinated by the early developments in flying, and became vaguely interested in Socialism. He had many friends, including Englishmen and Indian Muslims. He enjoyed sports; he was cox in his college boat and went mountaineering when he could. On one holiday in Norway he was nearly killed when climbing. In 1910 he gained a second-class honours degree and decided to go to London to the Inner Temple to study to become a barrister. By this time he was a handsome young man with black hair and a mustache. He always wore expensive fashionable clothes, went to fashionable clubs and parties, and all the social functions which the English upper classes usually attended.

In 1912 he was called to the Bar and after seven years in England returned to India, a qualified barrister. Later he looked back at himself in 1912 and said this: 'Less than ten years ago I returned from England after a long stay there.... I had imbibed most of the prejudices of Harrow and Cambridge, and in my likes and dislikes I was perhaps more an Englishman than an Indian. I looked upon the world almost from an Englishman's point of view ... as much prejudiced in favour of England and the English as it was possible for an Indian to be.'

His career in India made him much less sympathetic to the English government and her politicians, but he always remained as much English as he was Indian. He said himself, 'I have become a queer mixture of East and West, out of place everywhere, at home nowhere.'

Nehru's early career in India
Motilal Nehru had made his house, *Anand Bhawan*, one of the most important social centres in Allahabad. Here Nehru could meet anyone who was anybody in the town: politicians, writers, lawyers, journalists, businessmen and so on, but he was very bored. Allahabad was incredibly dull after London, and somehow he could not become absorbed in his work. He practised as a barrister for seven years without really making a name for himself. He talked about politics but never became involved.

His life began to change in 1916 when he was married. He was by then twenty-six years old and a very eligible bachelor. It was an arranged marriage. Motilal, after much thought, chose Kamala Kaul, the daughter of another wealthy Kashmiri Brahmin. She was only seventeen, tall, very beautiful and apparently very healthy. She was very shy and did not feel comfortable meeting strangers, as she had to as Nehru's wife. She was not very well educated and so spent some months with Nan and Betti's governess before her wedding. Gradually she grew to understand her husband and his work and shared in it (see page 39), but at first they had little in common. She had great courage and all who knew her admired her almost constant fight against pain and illness, for less than two years after her marriage it was discovered that she had tuberculosis, an incurable disease in those days.

The wedding was in Delhi, in February 1916. It was a lavish, splendid affair. Motilal hired a special train to take 300 guests from Allahabad. In Delhi a huge group of tents put up for the wedding guests was called 'the Nehru wedding camp'. Kamala quickly adjusted to the western way of life in *Anand Bhawan*. In 1917 her daughter Indira was born. She was to be the Nehrus' only child. A son was born in 1927 but died almost immediately.

Nehru had difficulty in communication even with those nearest to him. His aloofness can be explained both by his lonely childhood and by his training in England. There must have been many occasions when both Kamala and Indira felt rebuffed and hurt by his cold remoteness, despite his genuine love for them.

Nehru only became totally involved in Indian national politics in 1919. Like many other young Indians he was forced into action by the Rowlatt Acts (see page 25). When Nehru heard about Gandhi's plan for a *satyagraha* campaign in India, he wrote, 'I was afire with enthusiasm and wanted to join immediately.' Gone for ever was Nehru's feeling of boredom.

However, Motilal was unimpressed with Gandhi's ideas of *satyagraha.* Then came Amritsar, and Motilal finally changed his mind. Gandhi was right. Something would have to be done to show Indian feelings of hostility to British rule. Nehru wrote about Amritsar, 'I realised then more vividly than I had ever done before how brutal and immoral imperialism was.' In future years Nehru always referred to Amritsar as a turning point in his life, after which he was truly dedicated to the cause of Indian independence.

The year 1920 helped develop another side of his political philosophy. He had always been interested in the theories of Socialism. Now in 1920 he met Indian peasants for the first time and saw in practice what real poverty was. He decided that it could only be ended if India had a Socialist society. He wrote in his book *Towards Freedom* of his tour of the villages in the United Provinces. 'I was filled with shame and sorrow: shame at my own easy-going and comfortable life and the petty policies of our city which ignore this vast multitude of semi-naked sons and daughters of India: sorrow at the degradation and overwhelming poverty of India. A new picture of India seemed to rise before me, naked, starving, crushed and utterly miserable. And their faith in us, casual visitors from the distant city, embarrassed me and filled me with a new responsibility that frightened me.'

11 It was the memory of people poor and starving, like this woman, which always remained with Nehru after 1920

4 The struggle for independence 1920–47

Gandhi and civil disobedience
For nearly thirty years Congress and India were dominated by Gandhi. He made Congress a mass popular movement. He had an almost magical way of communicating with the Indian peasants. His appearance and way of life identified him with them, and he was able to explain political ideas by using traditional Indian words and symbols. His use of the words *swaraj* and *satyagraha* instead of self-government and non-cooperation made these political ideas clear and easily understood by the peasants.

As Gandhi became older it becomes more and more difficult to describe him adequately. His outwardly simple life was misleading. He was a great visionary and mystic but also a very astute politician with an excellent sense of timing and a deep understanding of the psychology of his opponents. Many regarded him as a saint, but some of his opponents thought of him as a trickster: Churchill described him as a 'half-naked fakir'. Even his most devoted admirers recognised an increasing crankiness in his behaviour. He was obsessed with his vow of chastity and to test his self-control he began the practice of having young girls share his bed.

There is no doubt that many Congress leaders could not accept all of Gandhi's ideas. The more westernised ones could see little point in wearing *khaddar* (homespun cloth), meditation or fasting. But they did as Gandhi wished for they recognised that he was the only man who could hold Indians of so many differing views together. They needed his courage, his leadership and his moral guidance.

Gandhi never ceased to urge the importance of *satyagraha.* He believed that violence would simply make the British stubborn and thus postpone independence. In 1920 Gandhi, demanding *swaraj* in one year, called for a massive civil disobedience campaign to back his demands. He asked for a mass boycott of everything British. He called upon lawyers to boycott the law courts; students and scholars to boycott British schools; politicians and public leaders to boycott the legislative councils; and voters to boycott the new elections which were to be held according to the 1919 Act (see page 25). The campaign culminated in a national *hartal* in November 1921 when the Prince of Wales visited India. Thirty thousand congressmen were arrested, including Motilal and Jawarharlal Nehru. Many schools shut down, bonfires were made of British cloth and only one-third of the electorate voted in the elections.

When the campaign proved ineffective Gandhi called upon the peasants not to pay their taxes. Then for Gandhi tragedy struck. Twenty-two policemen were burned to death in their headquarters in Chauri-Chaura. Gandhi was heartbroken and immediately called off the entire *satyagraha* campaign. Very soon Gandhi was arrested and charged with rousing his people against

12 A demonstrator calls for the boycott of British cloth. Notice in the crowd the Muslim flags with the star and crescent (later used in the flag of Pakistan) and the Congress flag with the wheel (later used in the Indian flag)

the British government. The judge was determined not to make Gandhi a martyr, so with great politeness he said, 'I sentence you to six years imprisonment; no hard labour, and if it is possible to release you before that date no one will be better pleased than I.' As Gandhi left the court surrounded by weeping women, he smiled, patted the heads of children and went off as to a party. He asked that there should be no violence; instead India kept a day of mourning, with shops and businesses closed.

Gandhi felt lonely in prison; he was allowed no visitors and could write no letters. His only friend was a mouse which he tamed with gifts of sour milk.

By the end of 1923 Gandhi was ill and rumours quickly circulated that he was being poisoned and was dying. In January 1924 he had an operation for appendicitis, which left him weak. He was released in

April. He was increasingly called *Mahatma* ('Great Soul'), the name he was to be known by for the rest of his life.

His reflections in prison convinced him that he had been right in ending his *satyagraha* campaign after the tragedy at Chauri-Chaura. He was determined that there must be no violence in the Indian independence movement. He realised that the Indian masses lacked the discipline, training and organisation needed for an effective campaign of non-violent disobedience. He decided to try to educate the masses after he left prison, and so retired temporarily from politics. He founded the All India Spinners Association with a branch in every district. This not only promoted the making of *khaddar* but acted as a political organisation. He went about India preaching non-violence and the need for strong self-discipline.

Nehru and Congress
The massive civil disobedience campaign of 1920 made Nehru think deeply about politics. He had already decided that following the constitutional path laid down by the British would get India nowhere. On the other hand he disliked the terrorism which had broken out in 1919. He accepted Gandhi's conclusions about the importance of non-violence and the way of *satyagraha*.

When Gandhi called off the campaign Nehru was arrested for the second time. He had been organising a picket of firms selling foreign cloth in Allahabad. He made the following statement in court: 'I marvel at my good fortune. To serve India in the battle of freedom is honour enough. To serve under a leader like M. Gandhi is doubly fortunate. But to suffer for this dear country, what greater fortune could befall an Indian, unless it be death for the cause. Or the full realisation of our glorious dream.'

Between 1921 and 1945 Nehru served nine prison sentences, adding up to nine years in all. On the whole he was not unhappy in prison. He spent much of his time reading, studying and writing. He often had his friends and relatives in prison with him, and they had the long discussions which he loved. He most regretted his separation from his wife and daughter.

When Nehru left prison in 1923 he found a saddened and disillusioned Congress. Gandhi was in prison and subsequently retired to his *ashram*, and without his direct leadership Congress split. One group, the *swarajists*, led by Motilal Nehru, favoured cooperation with the British. They took part in the elections of 1921 and won seats in the national and provincial Legislative Assemblies.

The *swarajists* really believed that they were doing something for India. The Legislative Assembly (which had over forty Congress members after 1924) repealed the hated Rowlatt Acts, and gradually protected Indian industries by putting high duties on imported goods like Lancashire cotton and

Japanese iron and steel.

Opposed to the *swarajists* were Gandhi's followers, who still urged total non-cooperation with the British and their constitution.

Jawarharlal Nehru was uncertain what to do; he loved his father and was dominated by him. But he also loved Gandhi and believed he was right. He tried to find a compromise between the two sides and showed great skill as a conciliatory mediator. But the split was not healed and there was only the most superficial unity in Congress until Gandhi returned to politics in 1928.

Nehru's move to a more revolutionary position was encouraged by a trip to Europe in 1926–7. Sadly the reason for it was a worsening in Kamala's condition. She had to go to Switzerland for treatment for her tuberculosis. Nehru enjoyed the opportunity for winter sports and as usual he read widely. In the periods when Kamala showed definite signs of improvement, Nehru felt free to go off on various trips. In 1927 he attended a Congress of Oppressed Nationalities in Brussels. The Congress was organised by Communists and Nehru made his first contact with orthodox Marxists. He was greatly attracted by their ideas of a classless society and by their rejection of Imperialism. With Kamala and his sister Nan he made a brief visit to Moscow in 1927, and liked the feeling of equality he found. He returned to India more convinced than ever that India needed not only independence but also a Socialist society.

Gandhi was upset by Nehru's apparently revolutionary ideas and wrote to him, 'I feel that you love me too well to resent what I am about to write to you. You are going too fast.' Gandhi went on to urge Nehru to start his own party. Nehru never did, although Gandhi periodically urged him to do so for the next twenty years. Nehru frequently disagreed with Gandhi but would never leave him. He needed him, he was a father figure for Nehru, and moreover Nehru knew that the independence movement could never succeed without Gandhi.

About this time another Congress hero emerged. He was a Gujarati lawyer called Vallabhbai Patel. He organised the peasants in the Bardoli area of Gujarat into refusing to pay their land tax, which had just been increased by 22 per cent. Eventually the government of Bombay gave way and agreed to a mere 7 per cent rise. Patel became very famous and received the title *Sardar* (leader). However, despite his popularity he was never a serious rival of Nehru. This was because Gandhi made it clear that Nehru was his political heir. Gandhi knew that Nehru was more revolutionary, less religious and more hot-headed than himself, but he believed that he was the likeliest person to draw young, radical and westernised Indians into Congress and keep them out of the Communist party (started by M. N. Roy in

13 A demonstration against the Simon Commission, 1928

1922). Moreover, despite what he said to Nehru, Gandhi had no doubts of his loyalty. He told his friends that as long as Nehru was President of Congress it was as good as Gandhi's being President.

The Simon Commission, civil disobedience, the Round Table Conferences and the Government of India Act 1935
When Nehru returned to India in 1927 he found Congress very angry. The British government had appointed the Simon Commission to visit India and to recommend future steps to self-government. Unfortunately the government made the terrible blunder of appointing no Indian to the Commission, and Congress, under Nehru's influence, decided to boycott it. Nehru also persuaded Congress, for the first time, to vote for total independence for India, with no links with Great Britain.

Congress organised mass protest demonstrations against the Simon Commission during 1928. Nehru and many others had their belief in non-violence tested very severely. In Lucknow, Nehru found himself in a procession being beaten over the head by policemen. Later he wrote, 'I felt half blinded with the blows and sometimes a dull anger seized me and a desire to hit out . . . but long training and discipline held and I did not raise a hand except to protect my face from a blow.'

At the December meeting of Congress in 1928 Gandhi returned to politics and united Congress as it had been in the early 1920s.

In 1929 the newly elected Labour government in England decided to try to redress the harm done by the Simon Commission by calling a Round Table Conference to discuss India's future. At first Congress happily accepted the idea of sending representatives to the conference. But Nehru, now President of Congress, had many doubts. He insisted on the following conditions: Congress was to have more representatives than any other power or group, Congress was to draw up the future Indian constitution, and all political prisoners were to be released. The British government rejected all these conditions.

At the end of its 1929 annual meeting, Congress declared 'war' on the British. 21st January 1930 was proclaimed as Independence Day and a rousing Declaration of Independence drawn up. 'We believe that it is the inalienable right of the Indian people . . . to have freedom and to enjoy the fruits of their toil . . . we believe that if any government deprives a people of their rights and oppresses them, the people have a further right to alter it or abolish it . . . India has been ruined economically . . . village industries have been destroyed. . . . We hold it to be a crime against man and God to submit any longer to a rule that has caused this disaster to our country. . . . We recognise however that the most effective way of gaining our freedom is not through violence.'

Gandhi decided it was time to launch another *satyagraha* campaign to back Congress. He believed that the Indian people were now more ready for a truly non-violent campaign, and decided to attack something which would be understood by all Indians: the salt tax. Only the government was allowed to make and sell salt and it was heavily taxed to raise revenue. It was a brilliant move: many poor Indians did not understand what independence was about, but they did resent the salt tax.

Gandhi announced that he would break the law by taking salt from the sea. He set off from his *ashram* in Ahmadabad and began a walk of 241 miles. It lasted three weeks and ended at the Arabian Sea. As he walked he explained to all the villagers he met what he was doing, and thousands joined him. Nehru met him at one of his stops. 'I saw him staff in hand, marching along at the head of his followers with a firm step and peaceful but undaunted look. It was a moving sight.' Gandhi and his peasants marched down to the sea carrying pots and pans which they filled with sea water. As night fell great fires were lit on the sea-shore

14 Indian women, followers of Gandhi, breaking the salt laws by evaporating salt from sea water

and the water was boiled until only the salt remained. Ironically the salt was inedible, but the imagination of the world was caught by the sight of 5 million people taking part in a series of totally peaceful demonstrations.

Soon the campaign extended to boycotting British cloth and liquor. One important result of the campaign was that Indian women came out in numbers and took part in the boycotts. Many were arrested and thus the campaign for women's rights became inextricably connected with that of civil disobedience.

Gandhi was again arrested, this time for failing to give evidence to the police. He was given five years in prison and another seven years for carrying a Congress flag. The judge's verdict caused a demonstration in every major Indian city. In Bombay 50 000 textile workers went on strike and Hindu cloth merchants proclaimed a six-day *hartal.* By the end of 1930 the government had arrested 60 000 Congress members (Congress estimated 90 000 had been arrested).

The first Round Table Conference started in November 1930. It failed because no Congress representatives attended. Gandhi had played the major role in the 1930 campaign. The Nehrus were not able to do as much. Motilal gave his house *Anand Bhawan* to Congress and renamed it *Swaraj Bhawan* ('Abode of Freedom'). Nehru was arrested again in May 1930.

One thing gave him enormous pleasure. From prison he watched his wife Kamala work with Indian women in organising the boycott of foreign liquor and cloth shops in Allahabad. Nehru was even prouder when on 1st January 1931 Kamala was arrested. Kamala's farewell message was, 'I am happy beyond measure and proud to follow in the footsteps of my husband. I hope the people will keep the flag flying.'

Nehru was worried because his daughter Indira was not having a normal upbringing, with both her parents so involved in politics and now both in prison, so he began to write a series of letters to her giving her his views on history and politics. These letters were later published and called *Glimpses of World History.*

Motilal was sent to join Nehru in prison. He was seventy and ill and became worse in prison. He was released to die and Nehru was allowed temporary freedom to be with him. Nehru's younger sister wrote, 'I do not think I shall ever forget the agony in Jawarharlal's eyes as he approached the sick bed of the father he loved so deeply.' After Motilal's death Gandhi became the father Nehru both missed and needed so much.

Gandhi was not in prison long. After the failure of the first Round Table Conference Lord Irwin, the Viceroy, decided to try to break the deadlock between the government and Congress. Gandhi was released and he and Irwin began negotiations. Irwin won the most concessions. Gandhi promised to call off the civil disobedience campaign and agreed to go to the second Round Table Conference in September 1931; Irwin promised to release all political prisoners. Irwin was much impressed with the peace that came to India after his agreement with Gandhi. There were very few incidents.

The second Round Table Conference was a failure. Gandhi claimed to represent all India, but his claim was disputed by the Muslims, the princes and the Untouchables. Also the new Conservative government, unlike its Labour predecessor, was not anxious to hurry towards Indian independence.

While Gandhi was at the second Round Table Conference, Congress at its annual meeting drew up the Karachi Resolution which stated what kind of society independent India would have. There was to be freedom of thought and equality before the law regardless of sex, caste or creed. There must be protection for regional languages; workers must have a living wage and limited hours of work and be allowed to form trade unions. There must be unemployment pay and old age pensions. Untouchability must be abolished. All were to have the vote and free primary education. The state was to own or control key industries, services and mineral resources.

This declaration was Nehru's first really important contribution to the independence

15 Gandhi visiting the Prime Minister at 10 Downing Street in 1931 during his stay in London

movement. His first reward for this Socialist declaration was the massive support for Congress in the elections of 1937.

Gandhi returned from the failure of the second Round Table Conference to find India ruled by a series of excessively severe ordinances which turned the country into a police state. He protested to the new Viceroy (Lord Willingdon). But the government showed its contempt for Gandhi and Congress by arresting him, Nehru and thousands of others. Then Congress was outlawed, its records destroyed, its funds confiscated and its building seized. Meetings and processions were barred and the arrests and imprisonments continued. (In the first four months of 1932, 80000 Congressmen and women were arrested.) Congress tried to continue its *satyagraha* campaign, but the absence of funds and leaders and police repression forced the members remaining free to abandon their efforts.

Then in August 1932 another blow fell. The British government announced that in any future Indian constitution there would be no less than twelve separate electoral rolls, including a special one for Untouchables. To be fair to the British, they were attempting to see that the voices and opinions of the Untouchables were heard in any future Indian Parliament. Indeed the Untouchables' leader Dr Ambedkar wanted the separate voting list to safeguard Untouchables' rights.

Gandhi had every sympathy for Dr Abedkar and the Untouchables but believed that their interests would not be served by their having their own voting roll, for this would separate them still further from the rest of the Hindus. Moreover, Gandhi so distrusted the British government that he believed that their motive for introducing separate voting lists was further to 'divide and rule' the Indians. To prove his deep concern, Gandhi began his famous 'Poona Fast' which was to last until death or until the British gave way and abandoned the idea of a separate voting list for Untouchables. Eventually the British did give way, and Ambedkar and Gandhi made the Poona Pact which pledged them both to ending Untouchability.

In 1934 Gandhi realised that his *satyagraha* had failed to bring independence. So once again he resigned from Congress and toured India, restarting old village industries, hand spinning and weaving, the hand pounding of rice, the hand grinding of corn, oil pressing and making *gur* instead of using factory sugar. He lectured everywhere on nutrition and correct cooking methods. As always he urged Indians to be clean and hygienic and thus regain their self-respect. He continually spoke against Untouchability and so irritated orthodox Hindus that one threw a bomb at a car in which he was travelling in 1934 (no one was hurt). Without Gandhi's campaign it is doubtful if Untouchability would have been made illegal by the government of independent India in 1950. Although Gandhi officially withdrew from politics both in the 1920s and 1930s, it must be emphasised that Nehru, Patel and the other leaders constantly sought his advice.

As for Nehru, he was only free for six

16 Nehru with his wife Kamala

months in the years 1931–5. Usually Kamala accepted his imprisonments calmly, but this was not so in February 1934. Nehru wrote, 'Kamala went to our room to collect some clothes for me. I followed her to say goodbye to her. Suddenly she clung to me and fainting collapsed.' Perhaps Kamala knew that her tuberculosis was worse and soon would kill her.

Nehru was finally released from prison in September 1935. Kamala was now very ill and Nehru took her to Switzerland, but her tuberculosis was beyond cure and she also had angina pectoris. She died on 28th February 1936.

Nehru found some solace in work. He was again elected Congress President in 1936. Congress had made a rapid revival after its collapse in 1932, and was now very strong. In 1935 the British government passed another Government of India Act. India was to be governed by a federal system. Each province was given full responsible government. All the provincial ministers were chosen by the elected legislatures and were responsible to them. The legislatures were elected by a greatly increased number of voters (30 million). Each province had a governor who could take over the provincial government, but only in cases of real emergency.

The central government consisted of a legislature elected directly by both the provincial legislatures, and the Viceroy and his council. Such vital matters as revenue, defence and foreign affairs were reserved for officials appointed by the British. This 1935 Act was very important because it formed the basis for the later constitutions of India and Pakistan when they became independent in 1947.

In 1937, under the terms of the new Act, elections were held in India. Congress decided to contest them. Nehru led his party and organised the election campaign with great energy. The Congress manifesto was based on the Karachi Resolution of 1931 (see page 39). Nehru enjoyed himself electioneering. He travelled 50 000 miles in five months, by train, aeroplane, horse, camel, steamer, canoe, bicycle and elephant. He worked twelve to eighteen hours a day, trying to hammer home a few basic points. 'Fight for Indian independence, build Congress into a mighty army of the Indian people organising to remove poverty, unemployment, social and cultural degradation.' Congress did well in the elections. They contested 1161 seats and won 711.

After the elections Congress governments were formed in eight states. They worked with reasonable efficiency and maintained good relations with the provincial governors. Congress politicians gained invaluable political experience, but Nehru was not happy with these achievements. There were not enough reforms. He wrote bitterly to Gandhi, 'They are trying to adapt far too much to the old order.'

The Second World War
In 1939 Great Britain took India into the Second World War without consulting Indian political leaders. As a gesture of protest all the provincial Congress governments resigned. Congress leaders were furious about the British government's action, although they were *not* sympathetic to Hitler's cause. Congress had in fact criticised both Hitler and Mussolini throughout the 1930s.

Nehru was tormented by conflicting loyalties. He hated Fascism and Nazism, but he did not want India to fight in the war

17 Gandhi returns to lead Congress, 1940. Here he is talking to some of the most important people in Congress. On the left is Sardar Patel and on the right, Mrs Pandit, Nehru's sister. The photograph was taken by Nehru

except as Britain's equal partner. Gandhi thoroughly understood Nehru's position and wrote, 'Though he cannot be surpassed in his implacable opposition to imperialism in any shape or form, he is a friend of the English people. Indeed he is more English than Indian in his thoughts and make-up.'

In 1940 Congress turned to Gandhi to lead them in another civil disobedience campaign against the British. They gave him complete power and he said, 'As soldiers we have got to take orders from the General and obey them implicitly. His word must be law. I am your General.'

First Gandhi chose some of his most trusted followers to offer symbolic opposition to British martial rule. Then he extended the campaign, and by the middle of 1941 14 000 Congress men and women were in prison.

In 1942, with the Japanese getting dangerously close to India, the British decided to negotiate with Congress. Political prisoners were released and a Commission, led by Sir Stafford Cripps, was sent to India. The Cripps Commission promised that India would be independent as soon as the war ended provided Congress would help with the war effort. Congress rejected the Commission's terms. They did not trust the British to keep their word, especially as only one year earlier the British Prime

Minister, Winston Churchill, had said, 'I have not become His Majesty's first Minister to preside over the liquidation of the British Empire.'

After the failure of the Cripps Commission Gandhi launched his 'Quit India' campaign. He said, 'I want freedom immediately, this very night, before dawn, if it can be had . . . Congress must win freedom or be wiped out in the effort . . . we shall either free India or die in the attempt.'

These were brave words, but Gandhi's campaign had little time to achieve anything. The British could not have a revolutionary situation in the colony nearest to the front line with the Japanese. With great speed all the Congress leaders were imprisoned. Gandhi was put in the Aga Khan's palace.

Kasturbai voluntarily joined him in his captivity. She died in February 1944. She and Gandhi had been married for sixty-two years. She had given Gandhi many lessons in non-violent non-cooperation, and she had come at last to understand what he was trying to do.

At the end of the war Gandhi's chief concern was *not* achieving independence. He judged, correctly, that in war-weary Britain public opinion certainly was not prepared to support a further war to keep India, and this fact, together with the election of a Labour government, meant that Indian independence would be quickly achieved. He was now chiefly concerned with preventing bloodshed between Hindus and Muslims and even more in preventing the partition of India.

Muslims and the Muslim League
The strength of Islam had always been sufficient to give Indian Muslims a feeling of belonging both to a group quite different to any other in India and also to an international brotherhood which cut across national boundaries. Until the coming of the British the Muslims had officially ruled India. Their conquest by the British shattered their confidence and made them less willing to cooperate with the British then were the Hindus. Gradually, however, Muslim teachers, doctors, journalists and lawyers emerged. They began to reform Muslim social customs and education and eventually founded the Muslim League in 1906.

The League's first action was to see the Viceroy, Lord Minto. They said, 'We Muslims' (there were at that time about 62 million) 'are a distinct community with additional interests of our own which are not shared by other communities.' Lord Minto promised them (in somewhat obscure language) that in any future political reforms the rights of Muslims would be safeguarded by putting Muslim voters on a separate electoral roll. Then they could elect members to represent their special point of view.

This principle of separate electoral rolls was put into the 1909 Act and was extended in those of 1919 and 1935. The central and provincial legislatures had a quota of Muslim constituencies in which all the Muslim electors of that area were placed for voting purposes. In the Punjab the Sikhs had their separate roll, as did the Christian electors in Madras.

Some critics feel that putting Muslims on separate voting rolls merely served to emphasize the differences between them and the Hindus. But it would be quite inaccurate to over-emphasise these differences. There were several attempts to unite the League and Congress and these were successful in 1916 with the Lucknow Pact. In this Congress conceded the right of Muslims to separate electoral rolls and this did much to allay their fears of Hindu domination. Together Congress and the League demanded Dominion status for India.

For many years the Muslim League only represented a small minority of Muslims. Unlike Congress it remained an upper- and middle-class intellectual movement. Its weakness was shown in the 1937 elections (see.page 42). Candidates sponsored by the League obtained only 5 per cent of the Muslim vote. Congress gained the majority of Muslim votes and thus claimed to represent *all* sections of the Indian population. The elections proved that after thirty years of separate electoral rolls, Indians were still not divided politically on grounds of religion.

This situation did not last long. The Muslim League had a remarkable new

18 Jinnah, on the left, talking to Sir Stafford Cripps, leader of the Cripps Commission (see page 43)

leader, Mohammed Ali Jinnah (1876–1949). He was in many ways the Muslim equivalent of Nehru. He was westernised, a London-trained barrister and a successful lawyer in Bombay. He certainly did not start his career as a Muslim fanatic. Indeed he regarded himself as a westernised Liberal and was a member of Congress as well as of the Muslim League. In 1921 Jinnah had left India and settled in England. He married an English wife and settled down to an English life. He only returned to India when his wife died in 1934. He soon became the leader of the Muslim League.

He fought the elections of 1937 on the understanding that coalition governments between the League and Congress would be formed. He was sadly disillusioned by Nehru, who made one of the biggest political blunders of his career; one which was to make almost certain the future partition of India. Before the election there had been a tacit agreement that in some areas there would be coalition governments between Congress and the Muslim League. After the election Nehru demanded such impossible conditions from the League that any cooperation between them was impossible.

There was some justification for Nehru's attitude. The League had done very badly in the elections and it was a weak movement. As Congress had many Muslims in its ranks Nehru believed that it was a truly national party. But he had made a serious mistake in treating Jinnah so arrogantly. Jinnah came to believe that the only alternative to British rule was government by a Hindu-dominated Congress. If the Muslims were to be saved the League had to be strengthened and made into a mass popular movement.

Jinnah was proud, ruthless and utterly determined. He was not a demagogue, but he could arouse Muslim fanaticism. He worked systematically to frighten Muslims with pictures of what a future Hindu-dominated India would be like. Over and over again he emphasised that Hindus and Muslims were separate peoples who could never live peaceably together. Repeatedly he proclaimed, 'Islam is in danger.'

The British declaration of war in 1939 gave Jinnah and the League a wonderful opportunity. When the Congress ministries resigned, the League called on Muslims to celebrate a 'Day of Deliverance'. In many areas Muslims took over the ministries left empty by Congress men, thus gaining power, political experience and the gratitude of the British for their 'loyalty'.

In 1940, Jinnah demanded, for the first time, a separate sovereign homeland for Muslims which he called Pakistan ('Land of the Pure'). Very few Muslims had wanted a separate homeland before this. The Viceroy promised that the interests of loyal Muslims would not be ignored in any future British plans for India. Certainly many British politicians considered that the Muslims deserved some reward for their loyalty to the British during the war. This contrasted favourably with the activities of Congress, which many British people felt seriously endangered the British war effort.

The strength of the Muslim League was dramatically revealed in the elections of 1945. It won all thirty of the seats reserved for Muslims in the central legislature with 86 per cent of the Muslim vote; and 507 seats in the provincial assemblies with 74 per cent of the Muslim vote. The only setback was in the North West Frontier Province where

Muslims backed by Congress were elected.

Jinnah interpreted these results as an overwhelming vote by the Muslims in favour of the creation of Pakistan. He was now in a position to be very obstinate and determined in his discussions with the British. Shrewdly he realised that even in 1945 the British were already half convinced of the need for partition.

Partition and independence
At the end of the war in 1945 Congress prisoners were released and almost immediately negotiations were begun about Indian independence. There was now a power triangle between the British government, Congress and the Muslim League. Negotiations dragged on through 1946 and nothing was settled: Jinnah decided finally to convince Congress and the British of the need for partition by calling for Muslim direct action. 15th August 1946 was chosen. This was interpreted by the Muslim Chief Minister of Bengal to be a call by Jinnah for *Jehad* or 'holy war' against the Hindu infidels.

Early on the morning of the 15th Muslim gangs waited in the streets of Calcutta. As each Hindu shop opened, the Muslims set upon shopkeepers, clubbing, stabbing and kicking them to the ground. The shops were looted and set on fire. English residents, unharmed by either side, witnessed horrible atrocities.

It was not long before the Hindu mobs came out to seek revenge. After a week of carnage throughout Bengal an estimated 16 000 had died and countless numbers were injured. In Calcutta the hospitals could not deal with all the injured, and the dead and dying were left in the gutters. Gradually the British army restored order.

Jinnah, who ironically hated mob rule, certainly had no idea how dreadful the great Calcutta killings would be. It must be noted, however, that there must have been some organisation behind the Muslim mobs. Many were armed with two-metre *lathis* which they could not have found accidentally. Jinnah must certainly bear the responsibility of calling for direct action without making it clear what form the direct action was to take. He deplored the killings but believed that his point had been made. Hindus and Muslims could not live together peaceably.

The great Calcutta killing was probably the turning point in India's progress to partition. After it, only Gandhi and a few of his followers were convinced that partition would mean more and not less bloodshed. Gandhi was heartbroken. He put himself on a starvation diet of 500 calories a day and set off to walk through Bengal. Everywhere he went he brought peace. He pointed out that in Calcutta Hindus and Muslims had died protecting each other, and hundreds had demonstrated, shouting, 'Hindus and Muslims are brothers.'

Looking back, the creation of Pakistan seems to have been almost inevitable. Some

19 A Hindu murdered by Muslims in Calcutta. They are holding lathis (wooden laths), lethal weapons in trained hands

of the events leading to it have been mentioned: Jinnah's revitalisation of the Muslim League, and the British government's desire to be just to the Muslims in return for their wartime loyalty. The total inability of Congress and League politicians after the war, either to reach agreement about the future or to work together in the interim government, convinced many Congress men that if India was to have a government which worked at all efficiently then the Muslim League members would have to go, and they would only go if there was a Pakistan for them to go to. The great Calcutta killing was the final straw for most of Congress and the British.

In March 1947 the British government sent Lord Mountbatten as the last Viceroy of India. Mountbatten had already met Nehru in Malaya in 1946. They became lifelong friends. They were both charming, vain, energetic and immensely enjoyed being aristocratic. Gandhi trusted Mountbatten, but Jinnah remained aloof and rather hostile.

Mountbatten had orders to settle the Indian problem before August 1948. He moved around India like a comet and decided that independence must come as soon as possible. He also decided that partition was vital because violence was breaking out, especially in the Punjab.

In 1947, as independence and partition drew near, Gandhi still protested against partition, but no one listened any more. So he decided again on individual action, again demonstrating that love and courage could overcome apparently insurmountable problems. Remembering the events in Calcutta in 1946, he returned there again. He made friends with Suhrawady, the Muslim leader who had not been entirely without responsibility for the events of the previous August.

Gandhi set up his headquarters in a decaying house in Calcutta in the middle of a slum area. He held public prayer meetings and frequently walked through the streets with Suhrawady to demonstrate the unity of Hindu and Muslim. Within twenty-four hours of Gandhi's arrival in Calcutta, the miracle had happened. Great crowds gathered outside Gandhi's house chanting, 'Muslims and Hindus unite.' The events of 1947 both proved and disproved the power of Gandhi's *satyagraha*. Wherever he went love overcame fear and hatred. But when he was absent, as in the Punjab, no one was morally strong enough to replace him. Gandhi himself was only too aware that he had failed to persuade many millions of the importance of non-violence. 'All is dark, all is dark,' he repeated over and over again.

Tension increased and Mountbatten feared that if independence was not achieved quickly there would be more bloodshed and a dreadful civil war. Top-level meetings were held; Lord Mountbatten flew backwards and forwards between Delhi and London; an air of crisis hung over the Indian capital.

20 Gandhi with Lord and Lady Mountbatten, Delhi, March 1947

Eventually on 3rd June the leaders of Congress and the Muslim League reached agreement. A new date was announced for independence and partition. It was to be 15th August 1947. There were only two months in which to divide up this huge land and resettle a vast population. It was an impossible task. Nehru said, 'It is with no joy . . . that I commend these proposals, though I have no doubt in my mind that this is the right course.' Nehru assumed that partition would *end* the bloodshed. He was wrong. Millions of others, however, must share the guilt and responsibility for the bloodbath which attended partition. Only Gandhi, who spent 1947 trudging the roads of Bengal preaching sanity, could carry a light conscience.

Frantic planning continued. The Indian army, which was under British command, had to be divided between the new Indian and Pakistani commanders. The safety of British residents had to be secured. The rule of the princes had to be brought to an end and, most complicated of all, the boundary lines between India and Pakistan had to be drawn.

All the Congress leaders were agreed that autocratic princes could no longer be allowed to rule in a democratic state. Moreover, the continued existence of hundreds of princely states meant that India could not properly be united.

Naturally the princes did not welcome the ending of their power, but most decided to make 'the best of a bad job' (see page 61).

Each prince had to decide whether his state was to belong to India or Pakistan. He was to take into account the religion of his people and the geographical position of his state. They had all made up their minds by Independence Day with the exception of the rulers of Kashmir, Hyderabad and Junagadh. The fate of these states is discussed in Chapters 5 and 6.

Other states were to decide in their provincial assemblies if there was any doubt about the country to which they were to belong. The Sind and Baluchistan voted for Pakistan. But the Punjab and Bengal were divided and so decided on partition.

Lord Mountbatten then appointed Sir Cyril Radcliffe to head a commission of four judges (two appointed by the League and two by Congress) to decide the exact lines of the boundaries in Bengal and the Punjab. This was virtually impossible to do fairly, especially as the Commission had only two months in which to finish their work. Inevitably Muslims were left in India and Hindus in Pakistan. Sir Cyril finished his task mentally and physically completely exhausted. His report was not made public until after Independence Day, but wild rumours started and there were mass movements of Hindus and Muslims into areas where they thought they would be safe. Many were killed, a dreadful warning of things to come.

Independence Day was 15th August 1947. From the countryside thousands poured into Delhi, in bullock carts, on foot or in grossly overcrowded trains. Everywhere there were waving flags, ceremonial arches and cheering crowds. Nehru made a moving speech dedicating himself to India. It was a day of triumph. India had gained her independence without a war. Nehru broadcast to his people: 'The appointed day has come, the day appointed by destiny, and India stands forth again after long slumbers and struggles, awake, vital, free and independent.' But the man who had done more than anyone else to achieve this victory was not in Delhi. Gandhi was in the festering Calcutta slums, mourning the deaths of those who had perished in the Muslim-Hindu clashes.

The new boundary lines were announced after the independence celebrations. The panic which had been growing since the Radcliffe Commission's appointment burst into mass hysteria as Muslims found themselves in India, and Hindus and Sikhs in Pakistan. For millions on the wrong side of the boundary their only choice was death or flight, for the majorities in India and Pakistan all too often found the solution to the problems of their minorities in mass murder. (However, many individual Muslims, Sikhs and Hindus risked their lives to save their friends of different religions.)

The situation in the Punjab was particularly bad. It was the Sikhs' traditional homeland, but now the Punjab was divided, with boundary lines cutting across the Sikhs irrigation channels; their holy places were on both sides of the boundary and members of the same family found themselves foreigners to each other. Many had hoped for a separate Sikh state, and hardly any were willing to tolerate partition. Traditionally warlike, the Sikhs decided to take up arms against the Muslims.

The Mountbatten boundary force of 55 000 was quite unable for a long time to restore peace in the Punjab. In the chaos following partition, about 12 million people became refugees from India to Pakistan and vice versa. Six hundred thousand were murdered, but mere numbers cannot illustrate the horror of those weeks: children and old people met horrible deaths, often preceded by mutilation and torture. Trainloads of refugees were butchered and the trains would arrive at their destination with 'A present from India' or 'A present from Pakistan' scrawled on the sides.

In September 1947 Hindu refugees poured into Delhi to seek vengeance on the Muslims remaining there. Nehru toured the streets and rescued some Muslims, including two children marooned on a roof top with a Hindu mob waiting below to murder them.

Nehru and Mountbatten decided to suspend the normal government because of the emergency. With Patel they set up an Emergency Committee. Nehru ordered the

21 Bodies in the streets, a sickeningly familiar sight in towns in Northern India and Pakistan in 1947, during Hindu/Muslim riots

police to shoot Hindu looters; it was an unpopular step but it restored sanity. He also banned all weapons in Delhi, wondering in anguish how it was possible for India to fall so far from the ideals Gandhi had set.

Meanwhile in Pakistan Jinnah did not become Prime Minister as expected. This post was taken by Liaquat Ali Khan. Jinnah chose the less arduous post of Governor-General, since he already knew he was a dying man. He died in 1949. Jinnah was truly the father of Pakistan just as Gandhi was the undoubted father of independent India.

Again and again in 1947 Gandhi visited places where rioting and murder were taking place, and restored peace by prayer, fasting and reasoning. In January 1948 he returned to Delhi, hoping to go on to the Punjab, but more rioting had broken out in Delhi so he decided to stay there for a while. He was now seventy-eight years old, but he began a fast unto death to stop the communal bloodshed in Delhi. The fast had the desired effect and peace was restored to Delhi.

Then Sardar Patel (see page 35) persuaded the Indian Cabinet to withhold money (550 million rupees) which India owed to Pakistan under the partition agreement. Gandhi was appalled at what he regarded as this most immoral act. Patel felt he was justified in withholding help from an enemy and went with friends to explain his position to Gandhi. After a while Gandhi raised his head and said with tears streaming down his face, 'You are not the Sardar I once knew.' Everyone was stunned, Gandhi had made his point and the money was paid to Pakistan. The Indian Cabinet also promised to protect the life and property of Muslims living in Delhi.

Patel urged Gandhi to accept police protection, for orthodox Hindus, infuriated by Gandhi's concern for Muslims, had threatened to kill him. Gandhi refused protection. He said his life was in God's hands and if he was to die at the hands of an assassin then he must do so without fear or anger.

At five in the afternoon on 30th January Gandhi, still weak from his fast, went to his daily prayer meeting in the garden of the house in which was was staying in Delhi. Supported by two of his grand-nieces he moved slowly across the lawn surrounded by little groups of people asking for his blessing. Suddenly a young man pushed his way through the crowd, bowed, pulled the two girls out of the way and, drawing a gun, shot Gandhi three times. Gandhi fell, blood

22 Gandhi, on his way to the usual prayer meeting in his garden

spreading over his spotless white *dhoti*. He lifted his hands in a gesture of prayer and called '*Rama, Rama*' ('God'). Some minutes later he died.

Gandhi's assassin was a fanatical Hindu who disapproved of Gandhi's championship of Muslims. If the assassin had been a Muslim there would undoubtedly have been a terrible bloodbath in Delhi.

Nehru broadcast to his people: 'Friends and comrades, a light has gone out of our lives and there is darkness everywhere. . . . Our beloved Bapu (Father) is dead; . . . The light has gone out I said and yet I was wrong for the light that shone in this country was no ordinary light . . . it will illumine this country . . . and a thousand years later that light will still be seen in this country . . . that light represented the living, the eternal truth, reminding us of the right path, drawing us from error, taking this ancient country to freedom.' Later he said to Parliament, 'A glory has departed and the sun that warmed and brightened our lives has set and we shiver in the cold and dark. . . . The only way is to dedicate ourselves to the great tasks he undertook. . . . Let us be worthy of him.'

Gandhi had died for his beliefs. In dying he united his people. Nehru and Patel had quarrelled earlier. Now Mountbatten told them that it was Gandhi's wish that they be reconciled. They embraced and the memory of Gandhi's death kept them together until Patel died. All Indians were united in their deeply felt grief. Gandhi was both a politician and a saint, a combination of roles almost unique in this century. He was truly the father of modern India.

5 Nehru's India

Nehru as a man and leader
Nehru is one of the great men of the twentieth century. His biographer, Michael Brecher, wrote, 'Few statesmen in the twentieth century have achieved the stature of Jawarharlal Nehru. As the pre-eminent figure in India's era of transition he bears comparison with Roosevelt and Churchill, Lenin and Mao. . . . Only Gandhi inspired greater faith and adoration among the masses. Only Stalin had greater power.'

It has been said that whilst all Indians could identify with Gandhi, most wished that they could be like Nehru, who was handsome, elegant and always well dressed. Whenever he spoke he did so without coarseness or maliciousness. He was frequently witty and very charming. He was very brave as can be seen from the parts of his career already described. Churchill wrote, 'Here is a man without malice and without fear.' He did endless favours for quite obscure Indians who sought his help, like an Indian Christian girl who wanted to marry a Pakistani. Above all Nehru was a leader who was honest to a fault and was quite uncorrupted by power.

Nehru was not, of course, a perfect man. He had an uncertain temper which he never completely controlled although his outbursts became fewer as he grew older.

He worked fantastically hard and was only able to do so because of his quite outstanding physical health and stamina. Even when he was seventy years old he got up at 6.30 and did his Yoga exercise of standing on his head.

In 1960 his principal private secretary wrote, 'Some sixteen hours a day has been the practice with him day after day . . . all these thirteen years. The members of his staff who are all much younger than himself have never been able to keep pace with him.' Even with his enormous work load, Nehru had time to follow some of his hobbies until his last illness. He loved reading, especially scientific books and poetry; he was very fond of animals and had four pet pandas and a tiger cub at one time in his garden; he loved hills and walking and riding, and flew a glider till he was over seventy; he also enjoyed playing cricket and watching and listening to Indian folk dancers and singers.

He occupied a position of immense power in India. He was Prime Minister, Minister of Foreign Affairs and Congress President. Frequently he took over Ministries after a Minister resigned and before a successor was found. This was a tremendous burden for any man; it would have been possible for him to have done all these jobs thoroughly if he had delegated some responsibilities to others, but this he seemed incapable of doing. He felt he had to attend personally to every minute detail. One writer saw him before an important conference, checking all the inkwells on the table, to see if they were full.

He was naturally a man who walked alone

and relied on no one. In the 1930s he had written, 'One must journey through life alone, to rely on others is to invite heartbreak.' His only friend was Krishna Menon, who had spent many years in England. Nehru did not feel very close to his other colleagues, and this too may account for him taking on such a huge work load. He has been accused of being aloof and distant; this may have been true on occasions, but it must be remembered that Nehru really did not feel that he was entirely at home in India.

Nehru's failure to delegate responsibilities had a bad effect. The more he did, the less his colleagues did, preferring to refer almost every decision to him. Time and time again foreign visitors would hear Indian politicians say, 'Well, this is my view, but Panditji knows best.'

Nehru suffered from having few people to talk to about his many responsibilities. As a young man he had had his father to rely on, then Gandhi. It is perhaps significant that his closest friend after 1947 was Lord Mountbatten, a member of the British royal family. In his last years Nehru treated his daughter, Mrs Indira Gandhi, as his confidante. She lived with her father and acted as his hostess and undoubtedly discussed many political problems with him. Gradually as her two sons grew up, she took a more public part in politics. She became President of Congress in 1959, and in 1966, the Prime Minister of India, after the very brief premiership of Lal Bahadur Shastri, who died suddenly that year.

Nehru was undoubtedly at his best with the Indian crowds, the peasants and the workers. Everywhere he went Nehru was greeted with *'Pandit Nehru Kijai'* ('Hail Pandit Nehru'). Some peasants would shout with joy, 'We saw him, we saw him.' Ironically, for he was not a religious man, Nehru was frequently greeted as a saint.

To the end of his life Nehru remained a complex man, and because of the contradictions in his nature he was able to appeal to a wide range of Indian opinion. The Indian author Krishna Kiripalani (in his book *Gandhi, Tagore and Nehru*) wrote, 'He is at once personal and detached, human and aloof, with the result that he now appears fond, now cold, now proud, now modest. An aristocrat in love with the masses, a nationalist who represents the culture of the foreigner . . . the very paradox of his personality has surrounded it with a halo.'

Sardar Patel
From 1947 until 1950 Nehru shared the leadership of India with Sardar Patel. Nehru was Prime Minister and Patel Deputy Prime Minister. Nehru was fifty-seven in 1947, but Patel was seventy-two. Patel was a brilliant organiser and administrator; some called him a genius. It was due to his efforts that Congress established an effective network of party groups all over India. He controlled Congress as Nehru never did, and

23 Nehru in the garden of Government House, Delhi, with his daughter and his grandson Rajiv, 1950

was able to manipulate the party in Parliament when certain laws needed to be passed. He was very conservative, but his support was vital to Nehru for he led the wealthy middle classes of businessmen and merchants.

Between 1947 and 1950 every important decision in India was made by Nehru and/or Patel. It was often difficult to know which decision was made by which man, but it is clear that Patel played a major part in the reorganisation of the Indian states.

Patel died in 1950 and Nehru was left the undisputed leader of India. He desperately missed Patel's administrative ability and India was never so well administered in future.

Refugees and the problems of religion

The great flow of refugees after partition (it was estimated that about 12 million fled, about 6 million in each direction) created many and lasting problems for both India and Pakistan.

Millions of refugees had to be found homes and work. Many had left all their possessions behind them and so had to be fed and clothed too. At one time India had 160 refugee camps housing, clothing, feeding and caring for the health of 1·25 million refugees. Unfortunately Hindu and Sikh refugees often left behind irrigated land much richer than the land left behind by the Muslims fleeing from India. Therefore quarrels over property and land have continued to bedevil relations between India and Pakistan.

The problems and the human suffering were so enormous that Nehru began to wonder if in fact partition had been the right thing to do. A year later he said, 'I do not know now had I the same choice how I would decide.'

However, India did very well in settling her vast numbers of refugees in the Punjab. The refugees accepted a lower standard of living and were helped by large government grants. With this help and their own hard work they have made the Punjab one of the most prosperous areas of India.

The problem of settling the refugees from East Pakistan (now Bangladesh) was more difficult, for West Bengal in general and Calcutta in particular are grossly over-populated. They were not able to absorb the extra millions of refugees. Anyone who has been to Calcutta, once the stately capital of British India, can never forget the terrible things they have seen there. The population is 6 million. One-quarter of these people live in what are called 'slums'. One-quarter have no homes at all and live on the pavements, cooking, eating, sleeping, and all too frequently dying there too. The infant mortality rate is 673 per thousand. In fact, the total death rate exceeds the birth rate, but the population continues to expand because of the migration of poor peasants from Bihar and particularly because of the flow of refugees from East Pakistan.

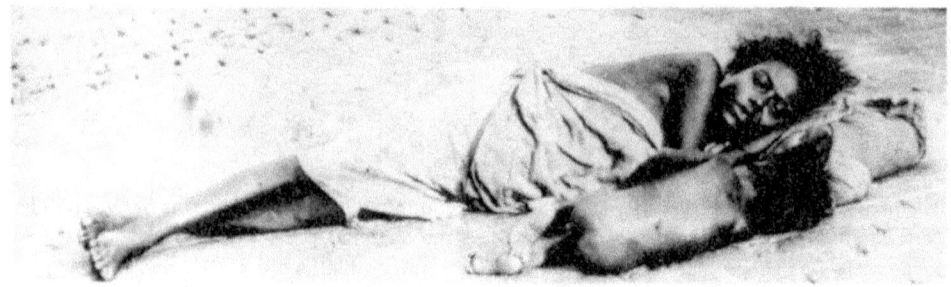
24 A starving mother and child lying on the pavement in Calcutta

In India, Nehru could not understand religious bigotry and its resulting violence. He was determined that India should be a secular state, but he never dismissed what was best in all religions. He wrote, 'Whatever raises a person above his normal level is good . . . provided he does not sit on somebody and force him to do it.'

Nehru had always accepted that Muslims were as Indian as Hindus and therefore entitled to the same rights. Immediately after partition he vowed to save the lives and property of all Muslims remaining in India, and in this he was remarkably successful. Muslims have held important positions in Indian life and there have even been Muslim Vice-Presidents of India. At the time of Nehru's death there were about 50 million Muslims living reasonably happily in India. There was little migration to Pakistan.

The new constitution
The new Indian constitution of 1950 was largely drafted by Dr Ambedkar, the Untouchables' leader, but it was illuminated all through with Nehru's philosophy and western liberal ideas. Practically it also owed much to the 1935 Government of India Act.

First of all the constitution established what kind of *state* India should be. It was to be a republic with a President and Vice-President. The first President was Dr Rajendra Prasad and the Vice-President Dr Radhakrishnan. These men were elected by Parliament. India was to be a federal state, which meant that each state had its own government which was responsible for the keeping of law and order, the police, local government, public health, education, health and irrigation. There was also to be a central government in Delhi with considerable powers; it controlled defence, foreign affairs, currency, banking, inter-state trade, food supplies, mineral resources and communications. The President could in emergency take over the government of any state and he did in fact do this five times from 1950 to 1960, the longest period being for one year.

India was to be a parliamentary democracy based on the British model. Parliament had 500 members each elected for five years by every adult man and woman. The Upper House of 250 members was to be elected by the state legislatures, plus twelve members chosen by the President. From the elected Parliament a cabinet was chosen and was responsible to it.

The constitution also was especially concerned with the rights of the individual. India was to be a secular, democratic, welfare state. The Constitution stated quite clearly, 'the State shall not discriminate against any citizen on grounds of religion, race, caste, sex or place of birth. . . . Untouchability is abolished, its practice in any form is forbidden.' In fact Untouchables were given special rights. They had seventy-six reserved seats in Parliament, and were given reserved places in educational establishments with generous grants.

Twelve basic freedoms were guaranteed to all citizens; among these were freedom of speech and expression, of peaceful assembly and association, movement and residence, worship and property. At the local village level the government was to be in the hands of the *panchayat* or village council.

The problems of the states
One of the most important tasks facing the Duumvirate was the full absorption of the princely states into the Indian Union.

The accession of the states had been achieved with three exceptions before Independence Day in 1947. The princes passed on to the Indian government the powers previously held by the British government (that is, foreign affairs, defence and communication), but reserved many personal privileges including large pensions. Many entered politics, some turned their luxurious palaces into tourist hotels, some bred camels for the army while others have become businessmen.

The second step to the full integration of the princely states was the establishment of democratic governments. Then they were fully integrated into the Indian Union, many small states being joined to others to make larger units.

The states which had not acceeded by Independence Day were Junagadh, Hyderabad and Kashmir. Junagadh was a tiny state in Kathiawar. It had a Muslim ruler but 86 per cent of the population were Hindus. The ruler chose to belong to Pakistan despite the fact that there was no land link between Junagadh and Pakistan and despite his Hindu subjects. Then the Indian army moved in; a plebiscite was held and 90 per cent voted for accession to India, which then took place.

The second state, Hyderabad, had a Muslim ruler but a largely Hindu population. It lay at the heart of India and could hardly belong to Pakistan. Actually the Nizam, its ruler, was more interested in making Hyderabad into an independent state. If he had been successful India could have disintegrated into dozens of similarly independent and possibly hostile states.

The Nizam had a large army and refused to give in to the Indian government's

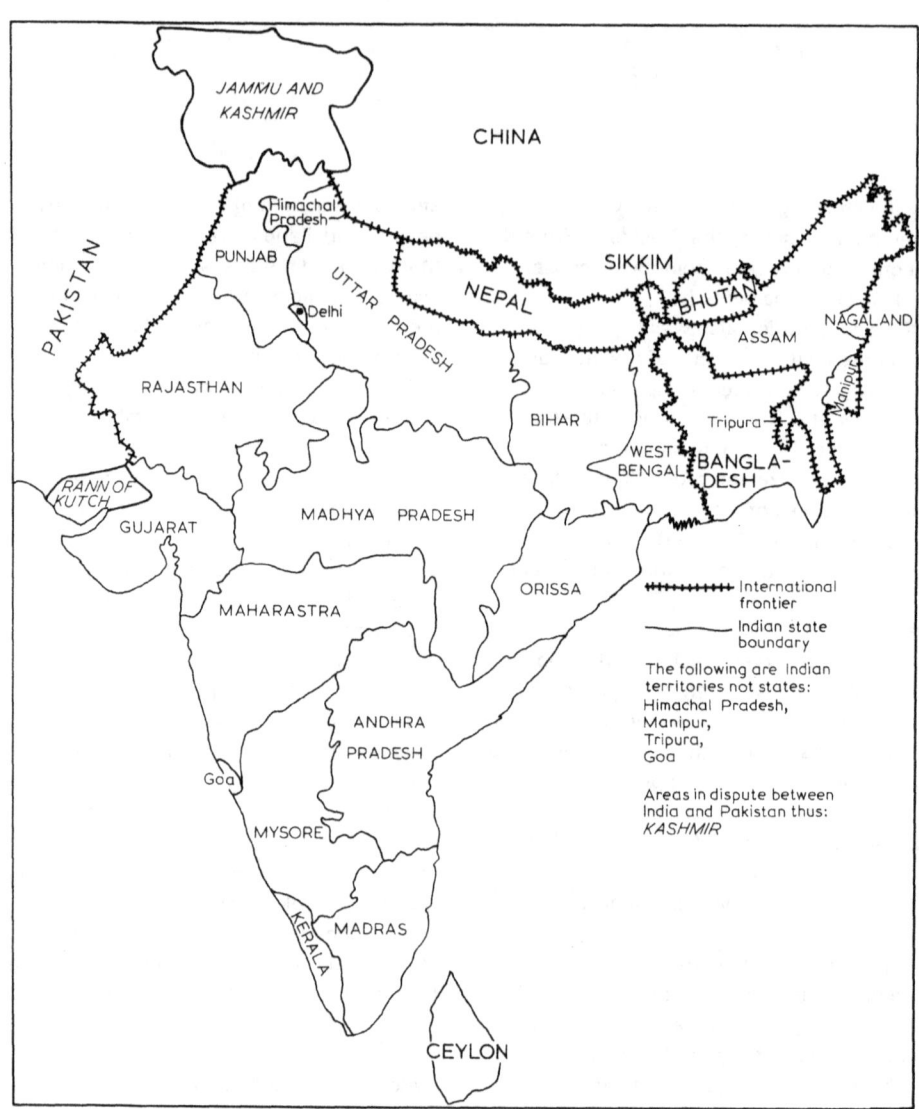

Map B India after 1947

requests for Hyderbad's accession. Then he imprisoned 10 000 Congress members, and there were allegations that his troops had tortured some strikers. So the Indian army invaded Hyderabad in September 1948 and the Nizam was forced to accede to India.* The army stayed until the elections of 1951 when a popularly elected government took over Hyderabad. The problem of Kashmir has still not been settled and has been a major source of disagreement between India and Pakistan (see Chapter 6).

As has been seen in Chapter 1, there are fifteen main languages in India and many more less important ones. A bitter struggle developed in Indian politics between those who wanted to leave well alone and those who wanted state reorganisation on the basis of language. Eventually in 1953 the government agreed to establish the state of Andhra for the Telegu-speaking people. This was the result of the Telegu leader Shri Potti Sriramolu fasting to death. The formation of Andhra opened the floodgates to demands for the formation of states based on language. By a new law passed in 1956, there were to be fourteen states based on language and seven territories.

When Nehru died in 1964 there were the following states in the Indian Union: Andhra Pradesh (for the Telegu-speaking people),

* The Nizam hardly suffered personally. He kept a revenue of 2·5 million pounds a year and a fortune estimated at 35 million pounds.

25 Nehru with a group of folk dancers from Nagaland

Assam (for the Assamese), Bihar (for the Biharis who, although separate from other Indians, are Hindu-speaking), Gujarat (for the Gujaratis), Kerala (for the Malayalam-speaking people), Madhya Pradesh (for Hindi-speaking people), Madras (where the people mostly speak Tamil), Maharashtra (for the Maharashtrians), Mysore (for the Kannada-speaking people), Nagaland (created in 1963 for the Naga people), Orissa (where the language is Oriya), the Punjab (Punjabi is spoken), Rajasthan (Hindi), Uttar Pradesh (Hindi) and West Bengal (Bengali).

In 1966 Haryana was created out of part of the Punjab for the Haryana people. Tamil Nadu is the new name for the old state of Madras with its Tamil-speaking people.

However, this reorganisation of the states did not inevitably mean that local loyalties became stronger than national ones. When Nehru died India was probably more united than ever before; Nehru himself had worked tirelessly for this end. He had been helped by the army, the transport services and communications. The Chinese war (see Chapter 6) had also helped to unite Indians in the face of an enemy.

The language problem
Until 1947 the language spoken or understood by the greatest number of Indians was Hindustani, which was an amalgamation of Hindi (which was spoken mainly by Hindus) and Urdu (which was spoken mainly by Muslims). Hindustani was one obvious way of uniting Hindus and Muslims. But after partition it became clear that Hindustani was unacceptable as India's national language. It was 'tainted' with Urdu, now Pakistan's national language. Congress decided that India's national language should be Hindi.

However, from the eighteenth century onwards, more and more Indians had spoken English. Admittedly only about 1 per cent spoke English in 1947, but the members of this select group also happened to be the rulers of India. English remains the language which intellectuals, politicians and businessmen from different parts of India must use if they are to understand each other. So there was and is a powerful group who wished and continue to wish to keep English as an official language in India. Indeed it became increasingly obvious that English could not be abandoned. As late as 1960 ardent pro-Hindi Congress members had to speak English in Congress meetings to make themselves understood.

Moreover, many men in Congress did not want to get rid of English. For instance, K. M. Pannikar, one of India's most distinguished civil servants, said, 'By going in for English, India joined a world community.'

English was due to be abandoned as an official language in 1965. By then Nehru was dead and the new Prime Minister, Shastri, decided to try to have Hindi used as the only official language throughout India. From then on documents like railway booking forms were to be filled in in Hindi. This decision produced chaos and rioting in the south with hundreds killed and millions of pounds of damage caused. Shastri gave up his attempt to abandon English and followed the path of compromise so often urged by Nehru. It was therefore again decided to keep Hindi as the major official language but to retain English too.

Indian democracy
Nehru was a sincere democrat and India's constitution reflected his beliefs. There are many ways of proving that India is a democracy; the press is free and foreign correspondents are unmolested and

uncensored. Perhaps one of the greatest tests of a democracy is to examine its elections, for there can be no democracy without free elections. Organising Indian general elections is a massive task. This was especially true of the first elections in 1951, when for the first time all adult men and women had the right to vote. It took a million workers to prepare for and organise the elections: new constituency boundaries had to be drawn and electoral lists made of all the 175 million voters.

This Indian general election was important, not only for India but for the whole non-European world, for it was the first free general election to be held in an independent non-white country.

The election took four months; 107 million voted. About 80 per cent of the voters were illiterate, so each candidate had to have a symbol on the voting paper. To prevent anyone voting twice a man or woman's thumb was pressed on to a pad of indelible ink.

The Congress party campaign was a one-man affair. Nehru campaigned with amazing energy. In forty-three days he travelled nearly 30 000 miles, making an average of five speeches a day. He pledged himself to an endless war on poverty and he also tried to get rid of the corruption associated with Congress (see page 67).

One of the greatest problems of the elections was communications (which was the reason for the vast amount of travelling done by the politicians). There were only 4 million radio sets in the country and of these there were only 600 000 in the villages. Only one village in ten had a Post Office. There were only 4 million newspapers printed each day. However, news did travel as newspapers were often read aloud in the villages, and sometimes educated villagers who had gone to the town would return to pass on all the news.

Congress won 362 seats in the Lok Sabha (the Lower House of Parliament) with 45 per cent of the votes. Thus it had a good working majority. Congress also had a working majority in all the states except Madras. The Socialists had $10\frac{1}{2}$ per cent of the votes but only twelve seats; ironically the Communists had only 5 per cent of the votes but twenty-seven seats in the Lok Sabha. Perhaps the most important result was the total failure of the extreme Hindu parties; together they polled less than 5 per cent of the votes. Democracy was seen to have worked in India.

The second general election was in 1957. Congress slightly increased its share of the votes both in Parliament and in the state elections. Nehru took little part in this election. Perhaps he was trying to see how Congress would get on without him.

The third election, the last before Nehru's death, was in 1962. Again Congress won. Again as in 1957 the Communist party was Congress's chief rival, and the Socialists lost votes for the second time. The

26 This shows something of the difficulty of communication in India:
a remote village in Marashtra, cut off by the mountains,
reached only by a rough track, and the only means of transport, the bullock cart

Swatantra party (see page 68) emerged as a national party with twenty-two seats in the Lok Sabha.

Nehru was the driving force behind establishing democracy in India; he certainly succeeded in establishing a parliamentary system of government and fair and free elections. But against these achievements must be set the inefficiency and corruption of so many government services, which made a mockery of the concept of democracy and justice. One Indian told the writer Alexander Campbell: 'A government clerk won't look at a poor man's application unless a fifty rupee bribe is attached to it. Politicians pose as snivelling saints while they plunder the peasants. In central India ten million people exist by eating the bark of trees. The cotton workers still sweat in foetid mills, children in coal mines do the work of pit ponies and women are put to mending roads . . . go and see the 50 million Untouchables still shut out of the temples and compelled to drink out of the ditch.' This outburst shows not only that Indians are their own sternest critics, but also that political equality cannot be equated with justice or economic and social equality.

Indian political parties
Congress
Congress had been united in its desire to drive out the British and achieve Indian independence, but it represented many different groups: those who followed Gandhi's rules for life; the peasants; the orthodox Hindus; the westernised Socialists; the landlords; the businessmen and factory owners; and the industrial workers. There were many quarrels between these groups, which made it difficult for Congress to have a coherent policy, and for Nehru to follow the policies he wished. Consequently many felt deep disillusionment that Congress did not achieve what it had promised in 1947.

Because Congress is so large, no other party offers an ambitious person the same opportunity to 'get to the top', and it has constantly been inundated with requests for jobs (often accompanied with a bribe). It is not surprising that Congress quickly gained a reputation for corruption.

Nehru was Congress's greatest strength and his personal popularity ensured that Congress remained the strongest political party in India. Congress was also the party which had achieved independence in 1947, and it could claim to have introduced the many reforms which were achieved in India after 1947.

The Socialist party
As early as 1948 the first split developed in Congress. It was feared that Patel's conservative influence would prevent Nehru carrying out the Socialist policies he had so long preached. This is indeed what happened and many Socialists were not

prepared to wait until Patel's death. Therefore they left Congress to form their own Socialist party led by J. P. Narayan. Caught between Congress and the Communist party, the Socialists often seem but a poor reflection of aspects of both.

Dr Ambedkar and the Untouchables
Dr Ambedkar also left Congress in 1951, resigning from his position as War Minister. He was protesting against the failure of Congress to pass (as yet) any laws protecting the Untouchables. He was never able to forget that Nehru was a Brahmin, although he himself had married a Brahmin doctor in 1948. Many Untouchables followed Ambedkar out of Congress. They did not form their own party, but adopted the Buddhist religion in 1956.

The Swatantra party
In 1959 one of Gandhi's oldest and closest friends, C. Rajagopalachari (Rajaji), left Congress to found the Swatantra party. Its name means Freedom. It is a Conservative party and represents private enterprise and big business. It opposes economic planning and the formation of a Welfare State.

Other right-wing parties
There are some extreme Hindu parties which oppose any alteration to Hindu traditions. They do not command much national support.

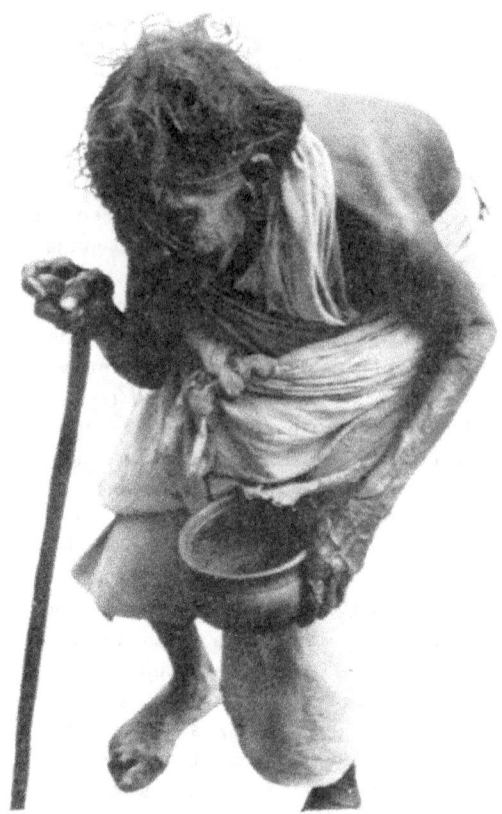

27 An old Untouchable for whom the reforms came too late

The Communist party
The Indian Communist party was started in 1922 by M. N. Roy. In the elections of 1957 the Communists won control of the state of Kerala. There were special reasons why Kerala had such a large Communist vote. It has a large number of well-educated people (frequently unemployed). About one-third of the voters were Christian and therefore perhaps not so traditionally

minded as the Hindus. It was clear that they voted Communist because they were disillusioned with Congress, which they believed had failed to introduce the hoped-for reforms in India. They expected great things from their new revolutionary government, but were disappointed. It could not act as a real Communist government because, according to the Indian constitution, it had no right to alter either the system of taxation in Kerala or the system of the private ownership of property.

One measure the Kerala government announced was the proposed take-over of all schools (including church schools), to come under state control. This caused massive anti-government demonstrations by Congress Catholics, Muslims, Hindus and the wealthy supporters of private schools. The demonstrations developed into riots which the Kerala government could not control, and the President established Presidential rule (see page 60). In the 1960 elections in Kerala the Communists won only twenty-nine seats. However, this was not the end of their political influence, and periodic disturbances have resulted in more Presidential rule in Kerala.

Another area where the Communists have won considerable power is West Bengal. This is almost entirely due to the misery suffered by the people of Calcutta, which is often attributed to the capitalist system.

Since Nehru's death the Communists have remained strong in areas like Kerala and West Bengal, but they have been repeatedly weakened by constant division and subdivision into quarrelling and hostile Marxist groups, some looking to Moscow for leadership and some to Peking. Many who know India well believe that she will never 'go Communist' because Hindus are both too religious and too permissive to make good Communists.

The land and the villages
Agriculture, the peasants and the villages are India's biggest problem, for about 80 per cent of all Indians (that is, 400 million people) live in the villages and make their living from the land. Moreover the peasants have not only to feed themselves but also the rest of the population, who live in the towns and cities.

Superficially some Indian villages look attractive. There are women in brightly coloured saris balancing water pots on their heads and surrounded by pretty children. There are houses painted with intricate geometrical designs, and there are flowers everywhere. But the picture is deceptive. Look closer and everywhere there is poverty: bones sticking through the skin; men, women and children dying of starvation or malnutrition. There is often no sewage disposal and no safe water supplies, and very few doctors and nurses to care for the sick or to control epidemic diseases. There is in fact a startling contrast between

28 An Indian village in the south near Madras. The simple thatch houses are shared by people and animals. The cattle are typically undernourished

individual personal cleanliness (both Hindus and Muslims wash very frequently) and public squalor. But Indian peasants have traditionally looked upon dirt and disease with a tolerance which is completely foreign to modern western man. This attitude, while helping the peasants to accept conditions and a standard of living quite intolerable to most Europeans, has also been a hindrance to change. Nehru was rude and intolerant of the villages. 'People with a cow-dung mentality living in a cow-dung country.'

In 1947 there was great inequality in the size of farms. All over India there were a few very rich men (called *zemindars** in north India) who had huge estates, but the great majority of farmers had only a few acres (the average was five) and these were frequently spread over a wide area. Many families had no land at all and formed a vast army of landless labourers (about 40 million in 1947). There was also a class of tenant farmers whose landlords were content to take a large proportion of the

* The *zemindars* were absentee landlords who had been given their estates by the British in return for tax collecting.

peasants' crops as rent but who did nothing at all to improve the land in return.

Peasant farming was primitive. The land was often ploughed with wooden ploughs and sown with poor-quality seeds. There was no rotation of crops, so the same land was used over and over again and became exhausted. The land was not manured because cow dung was dried and used as fuel. If the rains failed, so did the crops: if there was too much rain there could be terrible floods, with animals drowned and crops ruined.

Even in good years the peasants were very poor. Their greatest ambition was to grow enough to feed their families and have a little over to sell so that essentials like paraffin, matches, cloth and tools could be bought. There were other things, perhaps less essential to the western observer, which had to be paid for. Family weddings and funerals could cost vast sums of money. It is a father's sacred duty to marry off his daughter and give her a dowry and a large wedding feast. A son also has the sacred duty to cremate his father, and all the relatives have to be invited to the funeral feast. A peasant can spend as much as a year's income on a wedding or funeral. Inevitably peasants fall into debt and have to borrow from the local moneylender charging exorbitant interest rates. At the end of the 1960s it was estimated that despite improvements in local life at least one-third of all peasants were in debt.

One of the biggest problems was that of the sacred cows. No Hindu may kill a cow. Cows breed freely and the resulting stock is poor and diseased. The Indian cow's milk yield is the lowest in the world, and one American expert estimated that 90 per cent of Indian cows do not even pay for their keep. As there are two cows for every three people, cows and people are in direct competition for food.

Another great problem was underemployment. In 1947 an estimated 50 million families were unemployed for eight months of the year. This problem has increased along with the population. One result has been that more and more peasants have gone to the towns in search of work, thus creating a problem in the towns.

Since 1947 various attempts have been made to improve the lives of the Indian peasant farmers. One of the first actions of the central government was to abolish the class of *zemindars*. State governments passed over 200 acts applying to land reform. Rich landlords were bought out by the state govenments, thus making the tenants state tenants. Because of the landlords' compensation peasants had to pay high rents to the state, but these were gradually decreased and were much lower by the time of Nehru's death. After the land reforms about four-fifths of the peasants owned some land, but this could be as little as half an acre and few holdings were larger than five acres.

On the whole the land reform movement in Nehru's lifetime was a failure. There was no progress in the movements to establish cooperatives, to end the system of fragmented land holdings and to set up and extend credit facilities for the peasants.

However, there have been great improvements in some areas. For instance, the idea of the government's Community Development Plan was to form groups of about 100 villages (with a population of about 60 000 or 70 000). Each unit would have a group of specialists attached to it to advise on reforms in arable and animal farming, education, health and housing. The specialists' job was not to tell the villagers what to do in their villages but to discuss the peasants' problems with them and encourage them to reach their own solutions.

In theory the scheme should have been a triumph for self-help. But the specialists found their task very difficult. They found too many villagers did not understand or care about what the specialists were doing, and even when improvements were made the villagers often lost interest. More than half the new youth and women's clubs lapsed and died.

One of the basic reasons for this was the personality of the men of the *panchayat* (or village council). They were often traditionalist Brahmins who hated change, and because they were Brahmins members of the lower castes rarely dared challenge them.

Another reason for the weakness of the Community Development Plan was that there were not enough trained specialists to cover all India. Despite government campaigns and Gandhi's example, Indian students still preferred to study law or a subject which would not involve them in any manual work, such as agricultural science.

But despite its difficulties and failures the Community Development Plan did have many successes. During the first Five Year Plan, for example, 15 000 new rural schools were built and 1000 health centres. Visitors were much impressed by the contrast between improved and unimproved villages. Most of all they were impressed by the people's new feeling of hope.

A great many individuals and groups apart from the central and state governments have attempted to help the peasants. There are so many of these schemes that a complete book could easily be written about them. For instance, at Barpali in Orissa, American Quakers established a model village. When Bradford Smith visited Barpali he found irrigated fields of green crops, weavers again producing beautiful fabrics, healthy babies, and pure drinking water.

In the extreme south of India there is a project undertaken by a remarkable man known to the author, Joe Homan. Starting with a few acres and later moving to a much larger site, Joe has established a model farm

29 A village school in Marashtra. There is no money for chairs and tables for the pupils

built and worked by homeless boys. Some are trained as farmers, some as craftsmen and tradesmen, and eventually it is hoped that the profits from the farm will make it self-supporting, with enough over to give each boy a good start in life. Joe has received much help from Oxfam, from groups of schoolchildren all over Great Britain, and from the Indian government. He was given and asked to try out a new strain of maize seed, but he was asked especially to plant it by the road so that all who passed could see it. It grew and grew until it was about three times the size of everyone else's maize. Most of Joe's time is now spent seeing the endless stream of farmers who come to ask about his new seed strains, his irrigation systems and his tractor (which they can borrow). Although a modest man, he claims that his farm has produced an agricultural revolution in an area of up to fifteen miles radius.

Perhaps the most remarkable 'green revolution' took place in the Punjab. There Russian, British, American and Czech tractors can be seen at work. New strains of wheat seed, fertilisers and large irrigation works have helped the Punjabi farmers to surpass themselves. It can only be hoped that other areas will be similarly transformed in time to prevent increased agricultural production being overtaken by the ever-growing population. It is a race that Indian farmers must win if total tragedy is not to come to India.

30 Successful Sikh farmers in the Punjab harvesting the wheat

Economic development and the Five Year Plans

India was not an industrial state in 1947, but she had many assets which could help her become one. Water is one of India's greatest natural resources. There are at least six great rivers, and countless smaller ones which, if properly harnessed, could provide vast amounts of hydro-electricity and irrigate millions of acres. Most of India's other great natural resources were quite undeveloped. India has the largest iron-ore reserves in the world and the third largest manganese deposits; there are also large quantities of coal and bauxite, and four-fifths of the world's mica. There are smaller deposits of gold, chrome, lime, feldspar, and there is oil in Assam.

Gandhi had looked for the revitalisation of India through its villages. Nehru never disputed that the villages needed help, but unlike Gandhi he did not see that India had to choose between village revitalisation and industrialisation; he was absolutely convinced that India had to do both: the great problem was to decide how to allocate India's very limited resources.

Industrialisation was necessary. Firstly jobs had to be found for the ever-increasing number of unemployed who came to the towns looking for work. Secondly Indian manufactured goods could either be exported or used instead of imported foreign ones, and precious foreign currency saved. Thirdly industry would create the wealth which India needed so much for all the hoped-for social reforms. (In 1950 only 1 per cent of the population worked in industry, but they produced 15 per cent of the national income.)

At first Nehru was hindered by the conservative policies of Patel, but after Patel's death he found it easier to introduce a planned economy into India. He believed Socialism could solve India's problems of poverty, unemployment and low agricultural yields, but he was not prepared to force Indians into accepting Socialism. They were to be persuaded that Socialism would help them. India has remained both a capitalist and a Socialist country, and the new projects of the Five Year Plans have been financed by both private and public money.

In 1950 when Patel died, Congress set up a six-man planning commission with Nehru as chairman, which produced India's Five Year Plans. The first Five Year Plan (1951–6) was modest and cautious. Surprisingly it did not concentrate on industrialisation. The Indian government was to supply 24 billion rupees and private capital 16 billion.* Most of the money was assigned to agriculture and related developments (15 per cent on agriculture and community development and 17 per cent on irrigation and flood control). 26 per cent was to be spent on transport and communications, 11 per cent on power, 22 per cent on social services and housing, and 3 per cent on the rehabilitation of refugees, but only a total of 5 per cent on industry and mining.

Until 1951 only 17 per cent of India's water was used for irrigation. The plan envisaged many minor projects like the digging of wells and the building of water tanks and small dams, but there were many major projects too. In north India the Bhakra-Nangal Dam cost £130 million and irrigated $3\frac{1}{2}$ million acres of the Punjab and Rajasthan. The dam also generates 600 000 kilowatts of electricity. In Orissa the longest dam in the world was built, the Hirakud, at a cost of £50 million. When Nehru opened the Hirakud Dam he said (and shocked many Hindus), 'Orissa now has a new temple and it is a god for the whole country.'

Some of the results of the first Five Year Plan can be summarised. National income was increased by $18\frac{1}{2}$ per cent. Agricultural production increased by 10 per cent, and 5 million more tons of food than planned were produced. Industrial production increased by 40 per cent. Income per head increased by $10\frac{1}{2}$ per cent. Four hundred thousand acres were reclaimed from waste land and 16 million acres were irrigated. Eight thousand new schools were built and 68 million people were included in schemes for village improvements. Factories and two huge oil refineries were built.

However, India was very far from solving its problems. Unemployment was rising and the population was increasing fast. The planners decided to embark on a second,

* Ten million rupees are equal to £750 000. Therefore 24 billion rupees are equivalent to approximately £1800 million.

much bolder Five Year Plan (1956–61), putting greater emphasis on industrialisation.

The state was to spend 48 billion rupees (£3600 million), of which private enterprise was to provide half. 22 per cent was to be spent on agricultural and Community Development and irrigation; 9 per cent was to be spent on power, $18\frac{1}{2}$ per cent on industry and mining, 29 per cent on transport and 20 per cent on social services, housing and rehabilitation. The Plan needed £2500 million from outside India.

Steel was essential for the development of other industries and India had the necessary coal and iron ore, cheap labour and skilled middle classes. Three great steel works were built at Bhilai (with Soviet help), Durgapur (with British help) and Rourkela (with American help). Two steel plants were also built by private capital at Jamshedpur and Burhanpur. Around each plant was a new town for its workers. Now India produces the cheapest steel in the world, after Australia. However, India still only produces 1 per cent of the total American production.

The second Plan did not have the luck which attended the first. There was a period of very bad weather with floods, droughts and ruined crops and food stocks. The situation was so bad that cereals had to be imported and this proved to be a serious drain on India's foreign reserves, which fell by four-fifths. India could no longer afford industrial raw materials and machinery. At one point it seemed that the second Plan might have to be cancelled. Then in 1956 the World Bank created the Aid India Club. This provided adequate foreign aid to save the Plan.

By the end of the first two Plans, however, agricultural production had risen by 46 per cent and industrial production by 95 per cent. The national income had risen by 43 per cent and income per head by 18 per cent. Enough had been done in many spheres to ensure future developments: for example, every year since 1961 $\frac{3}{4}$ million more acres have been irrigated.

The great tragedy of the second Plan for Nehru was that the economies made in it resulted in limiting the extension of the Community Development Plan.

The third Plan (1961–6) was conceived by Nehru, but he was dead before it ended. It was bigger than the second Plan; the state was to spend 75 billion rupees and private capital was expected to provide 41 billion rupees. The aims of the Plan were as follows: 20 million acres were to be irrigated, bringing the total to 90 million, the production of food cereals was to be increased by 30 million tons (to 100 million), that of electricity from 5·6 to 12·7 thousand megawatts, that of coal from 55 millions to 97 million tons per year, that of iron ore from 10·8 to 30 million tons and that of steel from 4·5 to 7·5 million tons.

Again the Plan was not as successful as had been hoped. It had been made

31 The steel works at Jamshedpur

assuming a population increase of 2 per cent each year, but the 1961 census revealed that in fact it was increasing by 2·8 per cent each year. The Plan could not foresee the vast amounts of money needed for defence in the wars with China in 1962 and Pakistan in 1965 (see Chapter 6). There was also a cut in American aid. When Nehru died he knew that despite all his hopes and efforts there were still millions of Indians who starved and millions who had no jobs.

And yet the Indian people had achieved much. They paid (and pay) very high taxes so that state projects can be carried out. Compared with 1947 India had gone some way to becoming an industrial state in 1964. India now has the second largest textile industry in the world, producing 7000 million yards of cotton a year, and the largest jute industry. And there are also many more factories producing a huge range of goods from cars to planes and sewing machines to radios. India's progress is especially impressive compared with that of other underdeveloped countries. Many experts believe, however, that India needs much more foreign help if she is to really make rapid progress. Between 1949 and 1959 India received £1236 million in aid, but this is not a vast amount when the population of India is considered. Taya Zinkin* wrote, 'Indians, who make such heroic sacrifices to ensure a better future for their grandchildren, should get more aid than one and a half dollars per head.'

Population

India can never really end her dreadful poverty unless she controls her population explosion. Between 1891 and 1921 the population increased by 12 million; from 1921 to 1951 it increased by 169 million, and between 1951 and 1961 by 81 million, when it reached a total of 440 million. The population is now increasing by between 12 and 15 million people each year. At the present rate of expansion there will be 1000 million Indians by the year 2000.

* Taya Zinkin, *India*.

32 A young medical worker talks to an Indian mother and her children outside their home. This particular worker was checking whether or not the family had TB

The population has grown so rapidly because of improvements in medicine and hygiene, and the use of DDT which has reduced malaria, which used to kill a million people a year and make another 100 million ill. Wells have been chlorinated and vast programmes of vaccination and immunisation have been carried out. Much health education has been carried out through the new village health centres. The incidence of cholera, typhoid, hookworm and smallpox has been reduced.

Nehru tended to 'play down' the question of family planning. He said to Michael Brecher in 1956, 'The question of limiting the family is not the primary question . . . we have to make economic progress much more rapidly and we cannot wait for family planning to bring results. Also the rate of population growth in India is not high. . . . The point is that India can support a larger population given economic growth.' This underestimation by Nehru of India's population problem may be regarded in future years as his greatest failure as a leader, and one with catastrophic results for India.

Fortunately, even in Nehru's lifetime, many Indians felt that something had to be done quickly. Therefore family planning was budgeted for in the second Five Year Plan. Since Nehru's death far-reaching and intensive campaigns have been mounted urging the limitation of each family to two children. In 1964, the Deputy Chairman of the Planning Commission, Asoka Mehta, called for the sterilization of a million males each year. Propaganda campaigns have been carried out with the help of travelling puppet shows, massive posters and free gifts. But the campaign has a long way to go if it is to prevent the Indian population from doubling every century. Indians really love children and in most areas they can be valuable assets to the family labour force. There are also religious reasons for having children. In Hindu families sons are essential to carry out their parents' funeral rites and to care for their mothers if they are widowed. Most Indians, if asked, would say that their ideal family is three sons and one daughter. Certainly many women have gone to the family planning clinics asking how they can have *more* children. 'I have only three and I must have five.'

Education
The British did much for Indian education, but it mainly benefited the middle and upper classes. In 1947 only 15 million children had primary education, 3 million went to secondary schools and only 1 per cent went to university. The new constitution stated that there was to be free compulsory education for all children. This of course could not be provided overnight, but much progress was made. By 1960 the number of village schools had doubled and 35 million children (60 per cent of the total) had primary education. There were 18 million

in secondary schools, and a million students at university, college or research institutes.

The problem is particularly severe in rural areas. One-third of the population live in villages which are too small to support a school (i.e. less than 500 people). The children of these villages therefore either have no schooling or have to travel. There is also a shortage of teachers, especially of women, and many parents will not let their daughters go to school to be taught by a man.

There have been, and are, great problems in further education. It is very difficult for graduates to find employment. Many resent having to pay bribes to get jobs. Many more remain unemployed. This is partly because they choose to study for professions which are already overcrowded. There is still a great resistance to any form of manual work by 'educated' people. Even Gandhi was unable to kill the idea that manual work was degrading.

Old traditions and new ways
Gandhi had worked very hard to achieve the end of Untouchability and the equality of women. Neither group was really free in 1947. Then at last the Indian government made laws to see that both the Untouchables and women had the rights which Gandhi had wished. Untouchability was officially abolished in the new Indian constitution (but it should be noted the caste system was *not* abolished). Since then the Untouchables have been given much official help.

In the cities, on the whole, the law which makes it illegal to discriminate against Untouchables usually works. The law punishes offenders and in any case, in the anonymity of a city, it is difficult to guess to which caste anyone belongs. In the villages it is a different story. Everyone knows everyone else, so an Untouchable cannot pretend to be a member of another caste. Educated Untouchables tend to go to the cities and those who are left are thus deprived of their natural leaders and are less likely to stand up for their rights. The majority of Untouchables are landless and therefore depend on caste Hindus for work. In order not to displease them, they dare not draw water from the public wells or enter Hindu temples. If they do so they are likely to lose their jobs.

A writer named Alexander Campbell met the Government Inspector of Untouchables, Mr Vasagam, who led the Untouchables in one village into the temple and then into the local restaurant for a feast. The next day the restaurant owner was found smashing all the crockery which had been 'polluted' by the Untouchables and 'purifying' his floor by scrubbing it with milk.

Most experts on India believe that it will be a long time before Untouchability is ended, although it is clear that the lives of many Untouchables have been improved. There are some *advantages* in being an

33 A school for Untouchable women. In this training centre they learn handicrafts and poultry-keeping as well as reading and writing

Untouchable: for example, a certain proportion of government jobs and university places are reserved for them. In one extreme case in Mysore, 75 per cent of the population claimed to be Untouchables so that they could get university places for themselves or their children more easily.

Indian women have always been respected but through the centuries have become over-protected. They could not be free as long as they were married so young. In the 1920s 40 per cent were married before they were fifteen, and many before they were ten. Most girls could expect to be mothers before they were sixteen or seventeen, and the majority would have had at least six children before they were thirty.

According to the new constitution women were men's legal equals, but this was not enough. In 1955 the Hindu Marriage Act was passed. Girls could not be married before the age of fifteen, and bigamy and polygamy were made criminal offences. Divorce proceedings could be begun by women and provision was made for divorced women's financial maintenance.

In 1956 the Hindu Succession Act gave men and women, including widows, equal rights in the matter of inheriting money and possessions from relatives, and the Hindu Adoption and Maintenance Act gave women as well as men the right to adopt children.

At a wedding feast one guest grumbled to Alexander Campbell:* 'Formerly it was compulsory for a girl to be married before puberty. My niece, imagine it, is nineteen. Formerly even child widows were compelled to shave their heads and were forbidden to remarry. Now parents think nothing of marrying them off again as soon as is possible. In my day a wife treated her husband as a god. When he had done eating she ate what was left . . . wives prayed for long lives for their husbands and hoped to die first. If a husband died first everyone knew it was because his wife had sinned. Now wives sit boldly down with their husband at meals and they do not care a fig if a husband dies.'

The emancipation of women has been helped by education. In 1960 there were 200 000 at university compared with less than a dozen in 1900. Now an educated wife is a status symbol for a middle-class man, and so more and more daughters are being encouraged to take courses of further education.

Many women play a large part in politics and Congress reserves 15 per cent of its party tickets for women. India is now of course one of the very few countries with a woman Prime Minister, Mrs Indira Gandhi. Indian women have many important jobs. One woman doctor is a Squadron Leader in the Paratroopers. Another is the trade union leader of the Calcutta dockers. There are about half a million women in government service as nurses, teachers, civil servants, doctors and politicians.

These changes have helped to break down the joint family system in which all the members of a family of three or four generations lived together in one house. Young couples frequently had little life of their own, but today's educated young women have become too independent to accept their mother-in-law's dictation of their lives, and demand their own homes. Unfortunately this break-up of the family group does not help widows and old people who previously would have lived with and been helped by the joint family (indeed the great majority still are). But those without a family find life very hard in a land where there is little government social security.

* Alexander Campbell, *The Heart of India*.

6 India and the world

Nehru's views on foreign policy: India's general relations with the world.
After independence, Congress, deeply influenced by Nehru's views, defined the principles of India's foreign policy as the promotion of world peace, the freedom of all nations, racial equality and the ending of imperialism and colonialism. It was natural that India, having fought against an imperialist power for nearly thirty years and having suffered the indignities of being ruled by a foreign European race, should feel sympathetic towards the striving for independence of any non-white people in a European colony.

India wished to avoid military alliances, not only because she believed that they made the Cold War between Russia and the United States worse, but also because Congress suspected that the western powers, by establishing military pacts, were trying to return to the areas from which they had been driven as imperialist powers. Nehru and Congress were therefore very hostile to SEATO (South East Asia Treaty Organisation, 1954) and the Baghdad Pact (1955). Pakistan belonged to both and the Indian government felt that this brought the Cold War and the ex-colonialist powers together to the very doorstep of India.

India was not, however, inactive in attempting to make peace in troubled areas of the world. In 1949 India convened a conference which was attended by representatives of fifteen Afro-Asian powers, to discuss Indonesian independence. That this was achieved in 1950 was partly due to India's efforts. In 1954 Nehru took the lead in securing a truce in the French–Indo-Chinese war. Indian troops and ambulances under the United Nations flag have played an important part in peace-keeping activities in Korea, and in the Congo and Cyprus in the 1960s.

Nehru had great faith in the United Nations and for many years insisted on sending Krishna Menon, one of his most trusted friends, as Ambassador. Nehru realised that materially and militarily India had little power, but hoped that she would have moral influence through the United Nations.

Nehru hoped to unite the nations of Africa and Asia into a powerful bloc in world politics. In 1947 the first Asian Relations Conference was held in New Delhi, with twenty-eight Afro-Asian countries represented. Later, in 1955, Nehru was one of the leading statesmen at a meeting of twenty-five Afro-Asian powers at Bandung. The Bandung Conference was the high point of Afro-Asian cooperation. Disagreements and quarrels soon broke the apparent harmony between the Afro-Asian powers, and Nehru never succeeded in forming them into a third world power bloc.

In 1949 Nehru visited America and gained the impression that the only thing which mattered in America was money. He also disliked the way American coloured people were discriminated against. Later, in the early 1950s he was very angry about American arms supplies to Pakistan, which he felt directly threatened India. In turn the American government until the early 1960s tended to believe that no country could be truly neutral. If a nation was not positively on America's side (i.e. belonging to one of her military alliances) then she was hostile to the United States and virtually a member of the Communist bloc. This attitude irritated Nehru profoundly.

In contrast there were many aspects of Russian policy which he liked, and Russia was the only great power consistently to support India's case on Kashmir in the Security Council (see pages 87–8). In 1955 Nehru visited Moscow and in the same year the Russian leaders, Khrushchev and Bulganin went to India; relations between the two countries were very good.

Nineteen fifty-six was a year of crisis both for Nehru and the world. Nehru made some serious mistakes. The Suez war, when France, Great Britain and Israel took military action against Egypt, was roundly condemned by Nehru as an imperialist campaign. Very soon afterwards the Russians put down the Hungarian rising. Nehru was slow to condemn the Russians' action (perhaps he was frightened of losing Russian support for his case on Kashmir) and thus lost some of his reputation for fairness and lack of bias.

While Nehru's preoccupation with world politics did on the whole bring India moral influence and prestige, it also had some bad practical results, for it meant that Nehru tended to do too little about establishing really good and lasting relationships with his immediate neighbours. He was too complacent about India's security. He said rather smugly in 1954, 'I do not conceive of any kind of invasion or attack on India, not because of other countries' love of India but because it will bring them no profit.'

India and China
India shared a 2500-mile boundary with China, but because there had been no war between the two countries for many centuries and because the Himalayas provided a natural boundary, India expected no trouble. But China rapidly showed that she was not to be ignored. In 1950 she took over Tibet, a state on India's border, arguing that she was now reuniting the old China, and Nehru publicly accepted these arguments. Privately he sent two notes of protest to Peking. He feared the Chinese might turn their attention to Bhutan, Nepal and Sikkim, the border states whose friendship or neutrality was essential to India. The Chinese politely told him to mind his own business. Nehru thus could not claim that he was unaware that the Chinese could be hostile, but he was determined to forestall any aggressive intentions towards India by peaceful means. He deplored and continued to criticise the exclusion of

34 The border area between China and India. A lonely Chinese soldier stands guard

Communist China from the United Nations after 1949.

Then in 1954 a Chinese–Indian trade treaty was signed. Chou En-lai, the Chinese Prime Minister, visited Delhi and Nehru visited China. Together they agreed on the Five Principles of coexistence. There was to be mutual respect for each other's territorial rights, no aggression, no interference in each other's internal affairs, equality between them and peaceful coexistence. The cynical both inside and outside India greeted the Five Principles with scepticism. Certainly, unknown to the Indian public, the first border incidents had already started between India and China, only one month after the agreement had been signed.

The entire length of the border had either been defined by treaty or recognised by custom. Until the 1950s no Chinese government had challenged the frontiers. Then in the 1950s two areas of dispute developed. They were the North-East Frontier Agency (NEFA) and Ladakh which bordered on Tibet (see Map C). As far as India was concerned, the north-eastern frontier had been settled by the MacMahon line, a border drawn by the British in 1914. In 1956 Chou En-lai made it clear to Nehru that China would recognise the MacMahon line. The north-east frontier was a wild mountainous uninhabited area of little material use to either India or China. Ladakh was also wild and remote, but it was useful to the Chinese, who planned to build a road from Sinkiang to Tibet (see Map C) which would have to cross Ladakh. The fact that from 1957 the Chinese were able to build this road, without the Indian government being able to prevent them, shows that the Indians in fact had very little control over this area.

In 1959 the Tibetans rebelled against Chinese rule. The revolt was ruthlessly repressed and many Tibetans made the hazardous journey across the Himalayas to seek sanctuary in India. They were led by their spiritual head, the Dalai Lama. He was welcomed by the Indian government and his people were helped to settle in the foothills of the Himalayas. This was a grievous crime in the eyes of the Chinese; one which they found difficult to forgive or forget.

By 1961 China was claiming nearly 40 000 square miles of Indian territory. In October 1962 Nehru announced that the Indian army had orders to push the Chinese

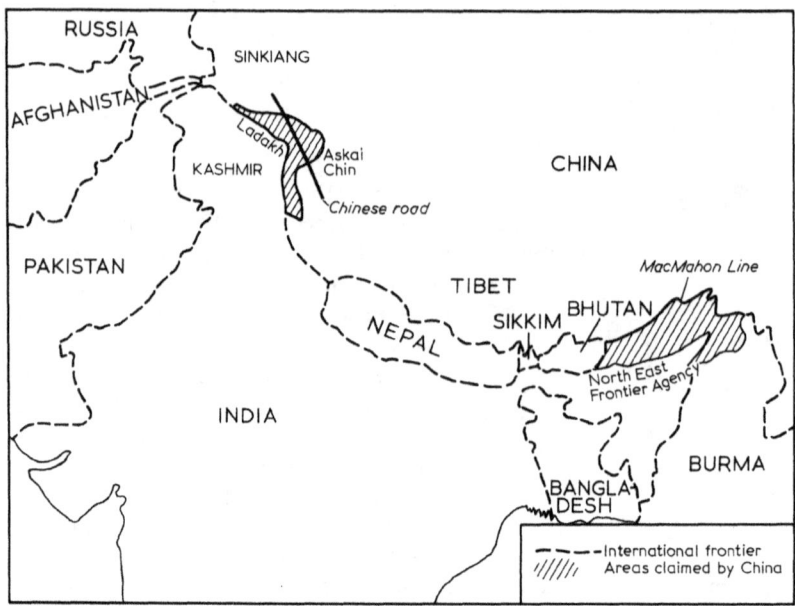

Map C The Indo-Chinese border dispute

back across the MacMahon line. India had already established forty new military points in the NEFA, and Nehru knew he was taking a risk with what could so easily be interpreted as an aggressive policy. In fact in October 1962 the Chinese denounced the Indians as aggressors and said they must be responsible for their 'crimes'. On 20th October the Chinese invaded India by pushing across the MacMahon line.

The Indians did badly in the fighting and by the middle of November 1962 had lost Ladakh and parts of the North-East Frontier Agency. Three thousand and eighty Indians were killed. There was a great upsurge of Indian national pride and determination to drive out the Chinese. Then, totally unexpectedly the Chinese withdrew from the NEFA, although they remained in the Askai Chin area of Ladakh to guard their road. Perhaps they were trying to show other Asian powers that China was more powerful than India, but this is only supposition.

The war had some sad results in India. The Defence Minister, Krishna Menon, was blamed for the failure of the Indian troops and was forced to resign. The government had to abandon its policy of strict neutralism and ask for American weapons; more disastrously, much of the Indian budget had to be spent on defence, when it should have been spent on development. Nehru himself must bear the largest share of the blame for India's humiliation. Despite warnings he had consistently underestimated the danger from China. A peace treaty was never signed between India and China, only a cease-fire.

India and Pakistan
It was inevitable that Indian–Pakistani relations should be bad, for the bitterness and hatred resulting from partition could not be forgotten overnight, especially as the flow of Hindu refugees from East Pakistan has continued since 1947. There were disputes about the property left behind by the millions of refugees and, more important, about the use of the waters of various rivers, especially the Indus, and of irrigation systems. There was also a disputed boundary in the Rann of Kutch (see Map B). But more than anything else Indian–Pakistani relations were poisoned by the quarrel over Kashmir. It must be emphasised that both countries were to blame for the bitterness between them.

To the visitor Kashmir is indeed an 'enchanted' valley which is unlike any other part of the sub-continent. It is surrounded by towering mountains yet the valley itself is lush, full of rivers and lakes and masses of flowers. The valley is 120 miles long and 80 miles wide at its widest point, and has always been cut off from India and Pakistan.

In 1946, in the Treaty of Amritsar, the British gave Kashmir with Jammu and Ladakh to Gulab Singh and his dynasty. The family ruled rapaciously and selfishly, caring little for their people, until 1947. At that date the Maharajah and the ruling classes (from which the Nehrus were descended) were Hindus, but three-quarters of the 4·5 million Kashmiris were Muslims.

The last Maharajah, Hari Singh Bahadur, wavered about whether to accede to Pakistan or India. There were good reasons for belonging to either, but perhaps he wanted to keep Kashmir independent with its revenue intact for himself. He was still undecided when, on 21st October 1947, Pathan tribesmen, looting, murdering and raping, invaded Kashmir from Pakistan. Three days later a terrified Maharajah acceded to India and asked for help. The accession was accepted and Indian troops were flown into Srinagar, the Kashmiri capital. The Pathan invaders, who now had the help of the Pakistani army, were halted by the Indians.

In 1948 India promised the United Nations that the Maharajah's accession was *not* irreversible and a plebiscite would be held once the invaders had left, but Pakistani troops have never left all of Kashmir and so a plebiscite has never been held, despite pressure by the United Nations Security Council.

In July 1948 the United Nations sent a five-man commission to Kashmir and a cease-fire line was established. This gave about two-thirds of the original Kashmir and Jammu (including the valley) to India and about one-third to Pakistan.

Nehru resolutely refused to accept that Pakistan had any claim on Kashmir despite its Muslim population. He said that there were already millions of Muslims living happily in India and that, if India renounced its claim to Kashmir, this decision could have the most disastrous effect upon the lives of Indian Muslims. It could well be that Hindus would seek 'revenge' for the loss of Kashmir in wide-scale killing of Muslims.

The Indian government has made great efforts to make the Kashmiris happy. The Indian part of Kashmir has much more self-government than any other Indian state. The maximum land holding is fixed at twenty-two acres; taxes have been reduced and rents kept low. There has been much spending on health and education.

Pakistanis believe that because 80 per cent of the Kashmiris are Muslims, the state should belong to Pakistan. Moreover there are practical reasons for Pakistan claiming Kashmir. All the Kashmiri rivers flow into Pakistan and are an important source of water for the irrigation of about 19 million acres. The roads which are open all the year round lead into the western Punjab.

Nehru attempted to establish better relations with Pakistan. He guessed that as India was so much bigger, Pakistan might well be secretly frightened of her neighbour. Therefore in 1950 he offered to sign a 'no war' declaration. He hoped to create an atmosphere in which problems like that of Kashmir could be settled, but the Pakistan government turned down Nehru's proposal (and did so again in 1956).

A year after Nehru's death relations became so bad that war broke out. Many were killed and much damage was done in the six weeks of fighting. Eventually the Russians arranged a peace treaty at a meeting at Tashkent. But the problem of Kashmir still remains unsettled.

Some problems have been settled between India and Pakistan. In 1960, due to the efforts and funds of the World Bank, the question of irrigation waters from the great rivers was solved, and in 1968 the disputed boundary in the Rann of Kutch was established.

India and the colonial territories in India
It was obvious that when India became independent in 1947, she would not tolerate the indefinite existence of French and Portuguese colonies in India. France owned Pondicherry and Chandernagore and Portugal had Goa (see Map A). (These territories covered only 200 square miles.)

After prolonged negotiations the French left their territories in 1954. Nehru believed that the negotiations with Portugal would ultimately have the same result. Following the Gandhian tradition, Nehru genuinely did not want to use force against the Portuguese, but the negotiations dragged on for more than ten years.

Much pressure was put on Nehru to use force. In 1961 he gave in, the Indian army moved into Goa and was soon in control. Ironically many Goans did not welcome their 'liberation' as they believed they were better off materially under Portuguese rule. Sadly,

35 Hindus and Muslims continue to coexist happily in Kashmir. Here side by side on the river Jhalum are the Muslim mosque on the left and the Hindu temple on the right

36 Abandoned Pakistani tanks in Indian fields. The farmers must move them before crops can be grown again

his actions over Goa diminished Nehru's international reputation. He had shown he could use violence and act aggressively.

India and the Commonwealth
For many years Congress had rejected the idea of Dominion status in the British Commonwealth. To the surprise of many Nehru accepted this status in 1947. There were practical reasons for India retaining its place in the Commonwealth; for example, in 1947 the United Kingdom owed India 2 billion dollars (her wartime debt) and Nehru had no wish to jeopardise the repayment of this money. Secondly India could not risk being totally isolated, especially in the dangerous days of the Cold War. Thirdly being a member of the Commonwealth gave India international status without her being a member of a military bloc. Fourthly India's foreign exchanges were tied up in the sterling area and the greater part of her trade was with that area too. Fifthly the Indian army relied on British-made weapons.

There were also deep psychological reasons why Nehru wished to retain links with Great Britain. He always recognised that he was as much English as Indian. It is probable that in the difficult years between 1947 and 1950, Nehru was constantly reminded of his ties with England by the close friendship and working partnership between him and Lord Mountbatten, the last Viceroy. Eventually India agreed to recognize the British monarch as Head of the Commonwealth but not as ruler of India. This formula has been copied by many African and Asian states since 1950, on the achievement of their independence. It is probable that the solution of Nehru and Mountbatten has made it possible for the Commonwealth to continue as a multi-racial group of nations.

37 Nehru with Lord Mountbatten

7 Epilogue

Nehru died on 27th May 1964. As Gandhi had personified the Indian independence movement after 1921 so Nehru symbolised independent India in the first seventeen years of her life. There was much to criticise in his leadership, but he was a very great man and a very great leader. He had held India together despite its vast religious, linguistic, caste and political differences. He had set it on a new course with a new constitution, laws and Five Year Plans all acting as signposts for the future. He was not really typical of India, but he stood for so many Indians' ideals. He showed his countrymen that a leader did not have to be self-seeking and grasping. It was clear that he held power solely in order to help his people. He succeeded in making Indians see the true beauty and greatness as well as the faults of the land he loved. Above all he gave Indians a vision of what India could one day become.

When Nehru died many millions of Indians, both rich and humble, felt that they were the poorer for his passing. His body lay in state and thousands (the police estimated half a million) filed past the body. Before the funeral procession set off Gandhi's favourite hymns were sung, 'Abide with me' and 'Rock of Ages'. Then Nehru's body, covered with the Indian flag, was carried off on a gun-carriage to the sacred river Yamuna. The police were unable to hold back the crowds and so on his last journey Nehru was surrounded, as he had been for most of his adult life, by crowds, the people's love, disorder, ineffectiveness and masses of colour.

At the place of cremation a helicopter showered rose petals on the gun-carriage. There was the sound of muffled drums and the body was placed on the funeral pyre. Mourners put sandalwood on the pyre, which was then lit by his grandson, Sanjay Gandhi. Then came the English part of the ceremony; a volley of shots and trumpeters playing the Last Post. The watching crowds shouted, *'Panditji amar rahe'* ('Panditji has become immortal').

Nehru's ashes were added to those of Kamala, which he had kept in his room for twenty-eight years. They were sprinkled into the Ganges at Allahabad.

Long before, in 1954, Nehru had written his own epitaph. 'If any people choose to think of me then I should like them to say, "This was a man who with all his mind and heart loved India and the Indian people. And they in turn were indulgent to him and gave him of their love most abundantly and extravagantly." '

A select booklist

by Norman Stone, ALA

Background

M. EDWARDES, *The Last Years of British India*, Cassell, 1963.

SIR PERCIVAL GRIFFITHS, *Modern India*, Benn (The Nations of the Modern World Series), 4th edn 1965. Maps, table, booklist. A description of modern India and the historical background to its development.

P. SPEAR, *The Oxford History of Modern India, 1740–1947*, Oxford (The Oxford History of India, Part III), 1965. Illus., maps, tables. An essential background book.

I. STEPHENS, *Pakistan*, Benn (The Nations of the Modern World Series), 3rd edn 1967. Illus., map, booklist. A companion to Griffiths's *Modern India*.

P. WOODRUFF, *The Men Who Rules India*, 2 vols, Cape, 1953–4. Illus., maps. Vol. 1, *The Founders*, covers the period from 1600 to the Indian Mutiny of 1858. Vol. 2, *The Guardians*, covers the period 1858 to the end of British rule in 1947. For the advanced student.

T. ZINKIN, *India*, Thames & Hudson (New Nations and Peoples Series), 1965. Illus., maps, booklist. A concise account of the development of modern India and her people.

General

G. ASHE, *Gandhi: a study in revolution*, Heinemann, 1968. Illus., map, booklist.

M. BRECHER, *Nehru: a political biography*, Oxford, 1959. Illus., booklist.

W. CROCKER, *Nehru: a contemporary's estimate*, with a foreword by Arnold Toynbee, Allen & Unwin, 1966. Illus.

M. EDWARDES, *Nehru: a pictorial biography*, Thames & Hudson (Pictorial Biography Series), 1962, Illus., table.

L. FISCHER, *The Essential Gandhi: an anthology*, Allen & Unwin, 1963. An anthology of the writings of Gandhi from the beginning to the end.

M. K. GANDHI, *Gandhi, an Autobiography: the story of my experiments with truth*, Phoenix, 1949. Illus.

P. MOON, *Gandhi and Modern India*, EUP (Teach Yourself History Library), 1968. Illus., booklist. A brief account of Gandhi's part in shaping modern India.

B. R. NANDA, *The Nehrus: Motilal and Jawaharlal*, Allen & Unwin, 1962. Illus., booklist. A joint biography of Nehru and his father.

D. NORMAN, ed., *Nehru: the first sixty years*, 2 vols, Bodley Head, 1965. Illus., map, booklist. Presenting in his own words the development of the political thought of Jawaharlal Nehru and the background against which it evolved. Includes 'significant passages from Nehru's writings, speeches, statements before the

court, press conferences, conversations, interviews and other documents, up to the founding of the Republic of India, 1950'. For the advanced student.
R. PAYNE, *The Life and Death of Mahatma Gandhi*, Bodley Head, 1969. Illus., booklist. An extremely detailed and thoughtful biography. For the advanced student.
G. TYSON, *Nehru: the years of power*, Pall Mall, 1966.

Index

A

Acts of Parliament
   Government of India Act 1919, 25, 32, 44
   Government of India Act 1935, 36, 42, 44, 60
   Indian Councils Act 1909, 21
Agriculture, 69, 70, 71, 72, 73, 75, 76
Ahmadabad, 22, 37
Allahabad, 28, 30, 34, 39, 91
Ambedkar, Dr, 40, 41, 60, 68
America, 83, 84, 86
Amritsar, 27, 31, 87
Asian Relations Conference (1947), 83

B

Baghdad Pact (1955), 83
Bahadur, Hari Singh (Maharajah), 87
Baluchistan, 51
Bandung Conference (1955), 83
Bangladesh, 9, 59, 87
Bengal, 21, 47, 51, 59
   West, 59, 63, 69
Bhutan, 84
Bombay, 21, 35, 38, 45
Brahmins, 7, 28, 68, 72
Brecher, Michael, 56, 78
British, the, 10, 11, 21, 40, 41, 43, 44, 46, 47
   Army, 47
   Government, 18, 22, 24, 25, 30, 33, 37, 39, 40, 47, 49, 61
   Parliament, 11
   Raj, 19, 21, 27

C

Calcutta, 24, 47, 49, 52, 59, 69, 82
Campbell, Alexander, 67, 80, 82
Caste system, 7–9, 28, 61, 80
Chandernagore, 88
China, 64, 77, 84, 85, 86
Churchill, Sir Winston, 32, 44, 56
Civil disobedience, 32, 34, 36, 38, 39, 43
Commonwealth, the British, 90
Communists, 35, 65, 68, 69, 84

Community Development Plan, 72, 76
Constitution of India, the new (1950), 60, 61, 64, 69, 78, 81
Cotton, 13, 21, 22, 34, 67, 77
Cripps Commission, the, 43, 44
Curzon, Lord (Viceroy), 21

D

Delhi, 30, 49, 52–4, 60
Democracy, Indian, 64–7
Dyer, General, 27

E

Economic Development, 74–7
Education, 13, 28, 39, 60, 61, 69, 78, 80, 82
Elections, 65, 69

F

Five Year Plans, 75–7, 91
Foreign policy, 83, 84
France, the French, 10, 88
Franchise, 25, 40, 41, 44, 45, 65

G

Gandhi, Feroze, 10
Gandhi, Mrs Indira, 10, 30, 39, 57, 82
Gandhi, Kasturbai, 14–16, 19, 44
Gandhi, Mohandas Karamchand (Mahatma) (1869–1948), 5, 8, 14–19, 22–7, 30–44, 47, 49, 51–7, 72, 74, 80, 91
Gandhi, Putlibai, 14, 16
Gandhi, Sanjay, 91
Goa, 88, 89
Gujarat, 22, 35, 63

H

Hindus, Hinduism, 5, 7–9, 14, 18, 28, 40, 41, 44, 45, 47, 49, 51–3, 54, 59–61, 65, 67–9, 78, 80–82, 87, 88
Homan, Joe, 72, 73
Hume, Alan Octavian, 21
Hyderabad, 11, 51, 61, 63

I
Independence, 5, 13, 21, 27, 31, 32, 34–7, 39, 41–4, 47, 49, 51, 52, 61, 67, 83, 90, 91
Indian Civil Service, the, 13, 21, 25
Indian National Congress, 19, 21, 22, 24, 26, 27, 32, 34–43, 45–7, 49, 51, 57, 63–5, 67–9, 82, 83
Industry and industrialisation, 13, 34, 39, 74–6
Irrigation, 13, 75, 76, 87, 88
Irwin, Lord (Viceroy), 39
Islam, 9, 44, 46

J
Jallianwallah Bagh, 27
Jammu, 87
Jinnah, Mohammed Ali (1876–1949), 45–7, 49, 53
Junagadh, 51, 61

K
Karachi Resolution (1931), 39, 42
Kashmir, 51, 61, 63, 84, 87, 88
Kathiawar, 11, 14, 61
Kerala, 5, 63, 68, 69
Khan, Liaquat Ali, 53
Kiripalani, Krishna, 57

L
Ladakh, 85–7
Land reforms, 71, 72
Languages, 5, 6, 28, 39, 63, 64
Legislative Assemblies, 25, 34
Legislative Councils, 11, 21
Lucknow, 36
Lucknow Pact, 45

M
Madras, 45, 63, 65
Mehta, Asoka, 78
Menon, Krishna, 57, 83, 86
Minto, Lord (Viceroy), 21, 44
Montague, Sir Edwin, 22

Morley, John, 21
Morley-Minto Reforms, the, 21
Mountbatten, Lord (Viceroy), 49, 52, 55, 57, 90
Muslims, 5, 9, 10, 18, 21, 28, 29, 39, 44–7, 49, 51, 52, 54, 59–61, 64, 87, 88

N
Narayan, J. P., 68
Nehru, Jawarharlal (Pundit) (1889–1964), 5, 28–32, 34–7, 39–43, 45, 46, 49, 51, 52, 54–6, 59–60, 63–5, 67–72, 74–8, 83–8, 90, 91
Nehru, Kamala, 30, 35, 39, 41, 91
Nehru, Krishna (Betti), 28
Nehru, Motilal, 28, 30–32, 34, 35, 38, 39
Nehru, Vijayalakshmi (Nan), 28, 35
Nepal, 84
North-East Frontier Agency, 85, 86
North-West Frontier Province, 46

O
Orissa, 63, 72, 75

P
Pakistan, 9, 42, 46, 47, 49, 51–4, 59–61, 63, 64, 77, 83, 84, 87, 88
East, *see* Bangladesh
Panchayat (village council), 8, 61, 72
Pannikar, K. M., 64
Parliament, the Indian, 40, 60
Parsees, 10, 18
Partition, 5, 21, 46, 47, 49, 51, 52, 59, 87
Patel, Vallabhbai (Sardar), 35, 41, 52, 54, 55, 57, 59, 67, 68, 75
Pathans, 87
Political parties (Indian), 67–9
Political situation in 1900, 10, 11
Pondicherry, 88
Poona Pact, 41
Population, 77, 78
Portugal, 88
Prasad, Dr Rajendra, 60

Princes and princely states, 10, 11, 39, 51, 61–4
Punjab, the, 25, 27, 45, 49, 51–3, 59, 63, 73, 75

R
Radcliffe Commission, the, 51, 52
Radhakrishnan, Dr, 60
Rajagopalachari, C., 68
Rajasthan, 63, 75
Refugees, 52, 59, 87
Religions, 7–10, 59, 68
Round Table Conferences, 36–40
Rowlatt Commission, the, 25
Rowlatt Acts, the, 25, 26, 30, 34
Roy, M. N., 35, 68
Russia, 83, 84, 88

S
Satyagraha, 18, 19, 22, 24, 25, 27, 30, 32, 34, 37, 40, 41, 49
Shastri, Lal Bahadur, 57, 64
Sikhs, 9, 10, 45, 52, 59
Sikkim, 84
Simon Commission, the, 36, 37
Sind, the, 51
Singh, Gulab, 87
Sinkiang, 85
Smith, Bradford, 72
Socialists, socialism, 29, 31, 65, 67, 68, 75
South Africa, 16–18
South-East Asia Treaty Organisation, 83
Srinagar, 87
Sriramolu, Shri Potti, 63

Sudras, 8
Suhrawady, 49
Swaraj and *Swarajists*, 21, 22, 24, 25, 27, 32, 34
Swatantra party, 67, 68

T
Tashkent, 88
Tibet, 84, 85
Tilak, 26, 27

U
United Nations, 83, 87
Untouchables, 8, 19, 22, 24, 39–41, 60, 61, 65, 68, 80, 81

V
Vaisyas, 8, 14
Vasagam, Mr, 80
Viceroy, the, 11, 21, 25, 39, 40, 42, 44, 46, 49, 90
Victoria, Queen, 11
Village crafts and industries, 13, 22, 37, 41
Villages, 69, 72, 74, 75

W
Willingdon, Lord (Viceroy), 40
World War, the First, 22, 25
World War, the Second, 42, 46, 47

Z
Zinkin, Taya, 77

For Product Safety Concerns and Information please contact our EU
representative GPSR@taylorandfrancis.com
Taylor & Francis Verlag GmbH, Kaufingerstraße 24, 80331 München, Germany

www.ingramcontent.com/pod-product-compliance
Lightning Source LLC
Chambersburg PA
CBHW052134300426
44116CB00010B/1900